P9-CMK-643

Classic
IRISH STORIES

BOOK SOLD
NO LONGER R.H.P.L.
PROPERTY

RICHMOND HILL
PUBLIC LIBRARY

SEP 23 2005

CENTRAL LIBRARY
905-884-9288

RICHMOND HILL
PUBLIC LIBRARY

SEP 26 2007

CENTRAL LIBRARY
905-884-9288

Classic
IRISH STORIES

TIMELESS TALES FROM IRELAND
AND OTHER GREEN SHORES

EDITED *by*

MICHAEL P. QUINLIN

THE LYONS PRESS
GUILFORD, CONNECTICUT
AN IMPRINT OF THE GLOBE PEQUOT PRESS

RICHMOND HILL
PUBLIC LIBRARY

SEP 23 2005

CENTRAL LIBRARY
905-884-9288

To buy books in quantity for corporate use
or incentives, call **(800) 962–0973, ext. 4551,**
or e-mail **premiums@GlobePequot.com.**

Special contents of this edition copyright © 2005 by
The Lyons Press

ALL RIGHTS RESERVED. No part of this book may be
reproduced or transmitted in any form by any means,
electronic or mechanical, including photocopying and
recording, or by any information storage and retrieval
system, except as may be expressly permitted in writing
from the publisher. Requests for permission should be
addressed to The Lyons Press, Attn: Rights and Permissions
Department, P.O. Box 480, Guilford, CT 06437.

The Lyons Press is an imprint of The Globe Pequot Press.

10 9 8 7 6 5 4 3 2 1

ISBN 1-59228-420-5

Printed in the United States of America

Book design by Claire Zoghb

Library of Congress Cataloging-in-Publication Data
is available on file.

To Ann Marie Quinlin, the bravest of them all

Acknowledgments

I am fortunate to have access to some of the finest libraries anywhere. I thank Steven Nonack, Mary Warnement, and the Reference Department staff at the Boston Athenaeum for their assistance in locating nineteenth-century materials, as well as Henry Scannell and Nancy Walsh at the Boston Public Library Microfilm Department. I am grateful to David R. Burke for creating the fantastic Irish Collection at the Lawrence Public Library, where I found several gems. I thank my former teachers who taught me to love Irish literature, especially the late Brother Patrick Sheekey, Benedict Kiely, Eavan Boland, and James Mays. Finally, my gratitude goes to Colette, Devin, Margaret, and Pat for their encouragement throughout this project.

Contents

CONTENTS

Introduction

Ireland's reputation as a wellspring of literary genius is hailed throughout the world. While other nations have cultivated visual arts, architecture, or even cuisine to define their civilizations, this race of storytellers has always used language to express the deepest dimensions of their cultural identity.

Classic Irish Stories offers a sampling of Irish literature through the ages, from short stories and novels popular in the nineteenth century to legends and ancient folktales of Gaelic Ireland. Like all good literature, the stories in this collection offer a mix of humor, love, drama, and tragedy as well as insight into the human condition.

The book opens with a beautiful story written in 1924 by Liam O'Flaherty, one of Ireland's greatest short story writers in the twentieth century. "Spring Sowing" is a meditation on the stark beauty and unforgiving environment of Ireland, as a husband and wife rise together on a chilly February morning to prepare their land for planting. The value of land to the Irish is a theme that comes up again and again in their literature.

Another recurring theme is the dual and often dueling Gaelic and Anglo sensibilities that have competed in Ireland for centuries. An undertow of tension suffuses these strained relationships: natives versus newcomers, tenants versus landlords, peasants versus aristocrats, Catholics versus Protestants, rebels versus soldiers, and so on. What comes out of these conflicts is the stuff of literature.

Bram Stoker, best known for his novel *Dracula,* captures the tension perfectly in his story "The Gombeen Man," in which the utter unfairness of the tenant-landlord relationship is exposed. "Some Parishioners," by George Moore, and "The Battle of the Berrins," by Samuel Lover, each speak to the authoritative reign that priests often had over rural Irish. And "The Faction Fight," by Frank Mathew, explores residues of a Celtic paganism in which shillelaghs and fisticuffs were used to uphold family honor in battles to the death.

Arthur Conan Doyle (author of *Sherlock Holmes*) reveals the complexity of Irish-English relations in the masterful short story "The Green Flag." A regiment of Irish soldiers, reluctantly fighting one of Great Britain's colonial wars in the African Desert, has lost heart in "fighting for the queen." As the British army is about to be slaughtered by Arabs, the Irish make a final rally behind the "little green flag with the crownless harp." Their valor seems pointless, since Britain's pejorative and racially charged views of Arabs and Blacks were equally applicable to the Irish, as Doyle surely knew, having been born in Scotland of Irish Catholic parents.

On a lighter note, strained relationships are fodder for Irish humor full of tender wisdom. "A Rich Woman," by Katharine Tynan, reveals a village mentality run amok as locals vie to win favor with a wealthy neighbor in hopes of getting into her will. "The Gaelic Concert," by Ellis N. Myles, pokes gentle fun at sacred cows in Irish society, including Irish language enthusiasts, country priests with urbane airs, Anglo-Irish patrons of the arts, and boisterous country folk who prefer Irish jigs to Italian operas. Chicago satirist Finley Peter Dunne puts a humorous slant on the earnestness of Irish Protestants and Catholics holding onto ancient grudges in his two stories, "Boyne Water and Bad Blood" and "The Freedom Picnic," which are narrated by Mr. Dooley, one of the most popular fictional characters in American literature.

As a counterpoint to Irish realism, *Classic Irish Stories* includes some favorite Irish legends and folktales that date back to the eighth century. These tales are part of a glorious oral tradition of recitation, song, and poetry that the Irish used as a means of preserving their history in the face of marauding invaders over the centuries. As Celtic scholars J. E. Caerwyn Williams and Patrick K. Ford note in *The Irish Literary Tradition,* Irish literature "remained very much alive where every literature ought to live—in the minds of the people."

In the late nineteenth century, this rich body of folklore—much of it still in the Gaelic tongue—was retrieved by an enthusiastic generation of scholars, writers, and intellectuals who set about translating and writing down these stories. This movement, known as the Celtic Revival, was led by William Butler Yeats, Douglas Hyde, Lady Gregory, and others, who helped uncover a treasure chest of Irish stories created by an ingenious Irish imagination centuries earlier.

Many of these stories share themes and structure that are common in folklore around the world. "The Wonderful Tune," by T. Crofton Croker, is a recognizable tale of a mermaid enticing a young man to leave the land and return with her to the deep ocean in the name of love. "The Red Pony," from William Larminie's *West Irish Folk Tales,* tells of a boy's arduous adventures of magic and supernatural encounters on his way to winning the girl he loves.

Larminie's version was transcribed from an Irish shanachie named P. Minahan of Malinmore, County Donegal.

Yeats's reflection on "Village Ghosts," from his collection *Celtic Twilight,* is less about actual apparitions as it is about how simple folk living in cottages on an island overlooking the edge of the earth interpret the mysteries of life. Lady Gregory's translation of "Oisin and Patrick" comes from the Fianna (Finn) Cycle and dates back to the eighth century. In it, Finn's son Oisin magically returns to Ireland from Tir na nog (Land of Youth) and finds that his family's authority has been replaced by Patrick and "armies of saints," a signal of Christianity eclipsing Celtic paganism in Ireland.

"Donald and His Neighbors" is taken from a collection of *Hibernian Tales* cited by William M. Thackeray in *The Irish Sketch Book,* published in 1842. Thackeray, a noted English author in his time, described *Hibernian Tales* as being "intended for the hedge school universities" and praised the "fancy, dramatic interest, and humour" of the stories. "Successful cunning is the great virtue applauded," he writes, "and the heroes pass through a thousand wild extravagant dangers, such as could only have been invented when art was young and faith was large."

Speaking of danger, "O'Reilly's Great Escape" recounts the true story of John Boyle O'Reilly's daring escape from a British penal colony in Australia in 1869, where he was serving a life sentence for sedition against the British Crown. After tramping through jungles and evading prison wardens hunting him down, O'Reilly escaped on a New Bedford whaling boat that eventually took him to America, whereupon he moved to Boston and became a noted poet and defender of the oppressed.

America emerges as a well-worn theme in Irish literature starting in the nineteenth century. The Promised Land is not often what it is imagined to be, as John McElgun shows in "James O'Rourke's First Day in New York." The innocent greenhorn is immediately conned upon arriving at Castle Garden and finds himself alone and penniless. That night he meets a stranger from "the ould counthry" who kindly takes him in, where upon the rags-to-riches tale—so popular in immigrant literature—begins to unfold.

"The Irishman Abroad," by George A. Birmingham, provides insight into how Irish immigrants made their way in America in the early twentieth century. "Those who went [to America] have always been the men and women for whom life at home seemed hopeless," Birmingham writes. "But in spite of the intolerable sadness of their going . . . there was some capacity for doing things. We can succeed, it seems, elsewhere."

In contrast to the Irish abroad, American author Kate Douglas Wiggin (best known for *Rebecca of Sunnybrook Farm*) depicts Ireland through American eyes in her novel *Penelope's Irish Experiences.* Three women travel around Ireland together in a manner that recalls the "harum-scarum gentry," a term that Yeats coined about certain Anglo-Irish writers who "did not take the country seriously." Still, this excerpt reveals an outsider's astute, if patronizing, observations about Irish life from Kerry to Belfast, where the "careless, genial, ragged, southern Paddy" is sketched in stark contrast to the "sturdy, prosperous, calculating, well-to-do Protestants" in the north.

Classic Irish Stories ends fittingly with Sarah Orne Jewett's classic short story, "A Captive Irish Maid," which straddles both Ireland and America. Cheerful and determined heroine Nora Connolly leaves her family and fiancé in the town of Kenmare to make her fortune in America and thereby save the precious piece of land so dear to her. As such, it's another variation on Liam O'Flaherty's opening story about the importance of land to the Irish psyche.

The selections in *Classic Irish Stories* represent just a modest glimpse of Ireland's tremendous literary library. In compiling the collection, I included stories that were quite popular in their time but tried to avoid duplication of works that have appeared in recent anthologies of Irish literature. My goal in choosing these stories has been to renew the general public's taste for literature that inspires, enlightens, humors, and entertains. Irish literature achieves all of that and more, as I hope these stories demonstrate.

Spring Sowing

[LIAM O'FLAHERTY]

It was still dark when Martin Delaney and his wife Mary got up. Martin stood in his shirt by the window a long time looking out, rubbing his eyes and yawning, while Mary raked out the live coals that had lain hidden in the ashes on the hearth all night. Outside, cocks were crowing and a white streak was rising from the ground as it were and beginning to scatter the darkness. It was a February morning, dry, cold and starry.

The couple sat down to their breakfast of tea, bread and butter, in silence. They had only been married the previous autumn and it was hateful leaving a warm bed at such an early hour. They both felt in a bad humour and ate, wrapped in their thoughts. Martin with his brown hair and eyes, his freckled face and his little fair moustache, looked too young to be married, and his wife looked hardly more than a girl, red-cheeked and blue-eyed, her black hair piled at the rear of her head, with a large comb gleaming in the middle of the pile, Spanish fashion. They were both dressed in rough home-spuns, and both wore the loose white frieze shirt that Inverara peasants use for work in the fields.

They ate in silence, sleepy and bad humoured and yet on fire with excitement, for it was the first day of their first spring sowing as man and wife. And each felt the glamour of that day on which they were to open up the earth together and plant seeds in it. So they sat in silence and bad humour, for somehow the imminence of an event that had been long expected, loved, feared and prepared for, made them dejected. Mary, with her shrewd woman's mind, munched her bread and butter and thought of . . . Oh, what didn't she think of? Of as many things as there are in life does a woman think in the first joy and anxiety of her mating. But Martin's mind was fixed on one thought. Would he be able to prove himself a man worthy of being the head of a family by doing his spring sowing well?

In the barn after breakfast, when they were getting the potato seeds and the line for measuring the ground and the spade, a cross word or two passed between them, and when Martin fell over a basket in the half-darkness of the barn, he swore and said that a man would be better off dead than . . . But before he could finish whatever he was going to say, Mary had her arms around his waist and her face to his.

"Martin," she said, "let us not begin this day cross with one another." And there was a tremor in her voice. And somehow, as they embraced and Martin kept mumbling in his awkward peasant's voice, "pulse of my heart, treasure of my life," and such traditional phrases, all their irritation and sleepiness left them. And they stood there embracing until at last Martin pushed her from him with pretended roughness and said: "Come, come, girl, it will be sun-set before we begin, at this rate."

Still, as they walked silently in their raw-hide shoes, through the little hamlet, there was not a soul about. Lights were glimmering in the windows of a few cabins. The sky had a big grey crack in it in the east, as if it were going to burst in order to give birth to the sun. Birds were singing somewhere at a distance. Martin and Mary rested their baskets of seeds on a fence outside the village and Martin whispered to Mary proudly: "We are first, Mary." And they both looked back at the little cluster of cabins, that was the centre of their world, with throbbing hearts. For the joy of spring had now taken complete hold of them.

They reached the little field where they were to sow. It was a little triangular patch of ground under an ivy-covered limestone hill. The little field had been manured with seaweed some weeks before, and the weeds had rotted and whitened on the grass. And there was a big red heap of fresh seaweed lying in a corner by the fence to be spread under the seeds as they were laid. Martin, in spite of the cold, threw off everything above his waist except his striped woollen shirt. Then he spat on his hands, seized his spade and cried: "Now you are going to see what kind of a man you have, Mary."

"There now," said Mary, tying a little shawl closer under her chin. "Aren't we boastful this early hour of the morning? Maybe I'll wait till sunset to see what kind of a man have I got."

The work began. Martin measured the ground by the southern fence for the first ridge, a strip of ground four feet wide, and he placed the line along the edge and pegged it at each end. Then he spread fresh seaweed over the strip. Mary filled her apron with seeds and began to lay them in rows, four, three, four. When she was a little distance down the ridge Martin advanced with his spade to the head eager to commence.

"Now, in the name of God," he cried, spitting on his palms, "let us raise the first sod!"

"Oh, Martin, wait till I'm with you!" cried Mary, dropping her seeds on the ridge and running up to him. Her fingers outside her woollen mittens were numb with the cold, and she couldn't wipe them in her apron. Her cheeks seemed to be on fire. She put an arm round Martin's waist and stood looking at the green sod his spade was going to cut, with the excitement of a little child.

"Now, for God's sake, girl, keep back!" said Martin gruffly. "Suppose anybody saw us trapesing about like this in the field of our spring sowing, what would they take us for but a pair of useless, soft, empty-headed people that would be sure to die of the hunger. Huh!" He spoke very rapidly, and his eyes were fixed on the ground before him. His eyes had a wild, eager light in them as if some primeval impulse were burning within his brain and driving out every other desire but that of asserting his manhood and of subjugating the earth.

"Oh, what do we care who is looking?" said Mary; but she drew back at the same time and gazed distantly at the ground. Then Martin cut the sod, and pressing the spade deep into the earth with his foot, he turned up the first sod with a crunching sound as the grass roots were dragged out of the earth. Mary sighed and walked back hurriedly to her seeds with furrowed brows. She picked up her seeds and began to spread them rapidly to drive out the sudden terror that had seized her at that moment when the first sod was turned up and she saw the fierce, hard look in her husband's eyes, that were unconscious of her presence. She became suddenly afraid of that pitiless, cruel earth, the peasant's slave master, that would keep her chained to hard work and poverty all her life until she would sink again into its bosom. Her short-lived love was gone. Henceforth she was only her husband's helper to till the earth. And Martin, absolutely without thought, worked furiously covering the ridge with black earth, his sharp spade gleaming white as he whirled it sideways to beat the sods.

Then, as the sun rose, the little valley beneath the ivy-covered hills became dotted with white frieze shirts, and everywhere men worked madly without speaking and women spread seeds. There was no heat in the light of the sun, and there was a sharpness in the still thin air that made the men jump on their spade hafts ferociously and beat the sods as if they were living enemies. Birds hopped silently before the spades, with their heads cocked sideways, watching for worms. Made brave by hunger they often dashed under the spades to secure their food.

Then, when the sun reached a certain point, all the women went back to the village to get dinner for their men, and the men worked on without stopping. Then the women returned, almost running, each carrying a tin can with a flannel tied around it and a little bundle tied with a white cloth. Martin threw down his spade when Mary arrived back in the field. Smiling at one another they sat under the hill for their meal. It was the same as their breakfast, tea and bread and butter.

"Ah," said Martin, when he had taken a long draught of tea from his mug, "is there anything in this world as fine as eating dinner out in the open like this after doing a good morning's work? There, I have done two ridges and a half. That's more than any man in the village could do. Ha!" And he looked at his wife proudly.

"Yes, isn't it lovely," said Mary, looking at the black ridges wistfully. She was just munching her bread and butter. The hurried trip to the village and the trouble of getting the tea ready had robbed her of her appetite. She had to keep blowing at the turf fire with the rim of her skirt, and the smoke nearly blinded her. But now, sitting on that grassy knoll, with the valley all round glistening with fresh sea-weed and a light smoke rising from the freshly turned earth, a strange joy swept over her. It over-powered that other feeling of dread that had been with her during the morning.

Martin ate heartily, revelling in his great thirst and his great hunger, with every pore of his body open to the pure air. And he looked around at his neigh-bours' fields boastfully, comparing them with his own. Then he looked at his wife's little round black head and felt very proud of having her as his own.

He leaned back on his elbow and took her hand in his. Shyly and in silence, not knowing what to say and ashamed of their gentle feelings, for peasants are always ashamed of feeling refined, they finished eating and still sat hand in hand looking away into the distance. Everywhere the sowers were resting on little knolls, men, women and children sitting in silence. And the great calm of nature in spring filled the atmosphere around them. Everything seemed to sit still and wait until midday had passed. Only the gleaming sun chased westwards at a mighty pace, in and out through white clouds.

Then, in a distant field an old man got up, took his spade and began to clean the earth from it with a piece of stone. The rasping noise carried a long way in the silence. That was the signal for a general rising all along the little valley. Young men stretched themselves and yawned. They walked slowly back to their ridges.

Martin's back and his wrists were getting a little sore, and Mary felt that if she stooped again over her seeds that her neck would break, but neither said anything and soon they had forgotten their tiredness in the mechanical movement of their bodies. The strong smell of the upturned earth acted like a drug on their nerves.

In the afternoon, when the sun was strongest, the old men of the village came out to look at their people sowing. Martin's grandfather, almost bent double over his thick stick, stopped in the lane outside the field and, groaning loudly, he leaned over the fence.

"God bless the work," he called wheezily.

"And you, grandfather," replied the couple together, but they did not stop working.

"Ha!" muttered the old man to himself. "Ha! He sows well and that woman is good, too. They are beginning well."

It was fifty years since he had begun with his Mary, full of hope and pride, and the merciless soil had hugged them to its bosom ever since each spring without rest. But he did not think of that. The soil gives forgetfulness. Only the present is remembered in the spring, even by the aged who have spent their lives tilling the earth; so the old man, with his huge red nose and the spotted handkerchief tied around his skull under his black soft felt hat, watched his grandson work and gave him advice.

"Don't cut your sods so long," he would wheeze, "you are putting too much soil on your ridge."

"Ah, woman! Don't plant a seed so near the edge. The stalk will come out sideways."

And they paid no heed to him.

"Ah," grumbled the old man, "in my young days, when men worked from morning till night without tasting food, better work was done. But of course it can't be expected to be the same as it was. The breed is getting weaker. So it is."

Then he began to cough in his chest and hobbled away to another field where his son Michael was working.

By sundown Martin had five ridges finished. He threw down his spade and stretched himself. All his bones ached and he wanted to lie down and rest.

"It's time to be going home, Mary," he said.

Mary straightened herself, but she was too tired to reply. She looked at Martin wearily and it seemed to her that it was a great many years since they had set out that morning. Then she thought of the journey home and the trouble of feeding the pigs, putting the fowls into their coops and getting the supper ready and a momentary flash of rebellion against the slavery of being a peasant's wife crossed her mind. It passed in a moment. Martin was saying, as he dressed himself:

"Ha! My soul from the devil, it has been a good day's work. Five ridges done, and each one of them as straight as a steel rod. Begob, Mary, it's no boasting to say that ye might well be proud of being the wife of Martin Delaney. And that's not saying the whole of it, my girl. You did your share better than any woman in Inverara could do it this blessed day."

They stood for a few moments in silence looking at the work they had done. All her dissatisfaction and weariness vanished from Mary's mind with the delicious feeling of comfort that overcame her at having done this work with her husband. They had done it together. They had planted seeds in the earth. The next day and the next and all their lives, when spring came they would have to bend their backs and do it until their hands and bones got twisted with rheumatism. But night would always bring sleep and forgetfulness.

As they walked home slowly Martin walked in front with another peasant talking about the sowing, and Mary walked behind, with her eyes on the ground, thinking.

Cows were lowing at a distance.

The Faction Fight

[FRANK MATHEW]

In the heart of the Connemara Highlands, Carrala Valley hides in a triangle of mountains. Carrala Village lies in the corner of it towards Loch Ina, and Aughavanna in the corner nearest Kylemore. Aughavanna is a wreck now: if you were to look for it you would see only a cluster of walls grown over by ferns and nettles; but in those remote times, before the Great Famine, when no English was spoken in the Valley, there was no place more renowned for wild fun and fighting; and when its men were to be at a fair, every able-bodied man in the countryside took his *kippeen*—his cudgel—from its place in the chimney, and went out to do battle with a glad heart.

Long Mat Murnane was the king of Aughavanna. There was no grander sight than Mat smashing his way through a forest of *kippeens,* with his enemies staggering back to the right and left of him; there was no sweeter sound than his voice, clear as a bell, full of triumph and gladness, shouting, "Hurroo! whoop! Aughavanna for ever!" Where his *kippeen* flickered in the air his followers charged after, and the enemy rushed to meet him, for it was an honor to take a broken head from him.

But Carrala Fair was the black day for him. That day Carrala swarmed with men—fishers from the near coast, dwellers in lonely huts by the black lakes, or in tiny ragged villages under the shadow of the mountains, or in cabins on the hillsides—every little town for miles, by river or seashore or mountain-built, was emptied. The fame of the Aughavanna men was their ruin, for they were known to fight so well that every one was dying to fight them. The Joyces sided against them; Black Michael Joyce had a farm in the third corner of the Valley, just where the road through the bog from Aughavanna (the road with the cross by it) meets the high-road to Leenane, so his kin mustered in force. Now Black Michael, "Meehul Dhu," was Long Mat's rival; though smaller he was near as deadly in fight, and in dancing no man could touch him, for it was said he could jump a yard into the air and kick himself behind with his heels in doing it.

The business of the Fair had been hurried so as to leave the more time for pleasure, and by five of the afternoon every man was mad for the battle. Why, you could scarcely have moved in Callanan's Field out beyond the churchyard at the end of the Village, it was so packed with men—more than five hundred were there, and you could not have heard yourself speak, for they were jumping and dancing, tossing their *caubeens,* and shouting themselves hoarse and deaf—"Hurroo for Carrala!" "Whoop for Augha-vanna!" Around them a mob of women, old men and children, looked on breathlessly. It was dull weather, and the mists had crept half-way down the dark mountain walls, as if to have a nearer look at the fight.

As the chapel clock struck five, Long Mat Mur-nane gave the signal. Down the Village he came, rejoicing in his strength, out between the two last houses, past the churchyard and into Callanan's Field; he looked every inch a king; his *kippeen* was ready, his frieze coat was off, with his left hand he trailed it behind him holding it by the sleeve, while with a great voice he shouted—in Irish—"Where's the Carrala man that dare touch my coat? Where's the cowardly scoundrel that dare look crooked at it?"

In a moment Black Michael Joyce was trailing his own coat behind him, and rushed forward, with a mighty cry, "Where's the face of a trembling Augha-vanna man?" In a moment their *kippeens* clashed; in another, hundreds of *kippeens* crashed together, and the grandest fight ever fought in Connemara raged over Callanan's Field. After the first roar of defiance the men had to keep their breath for the hitting, so the shout of triumph and the groan as one fell were the only sounds that broke the music of the *kippeens* clashing and clicking on one another, or striking home with a thud.

Never was Long Mat nobler: he rushed ravaging through the enemy, shattering their ranks and their heads; no man could withstand him; Red Callanan of Carrala went down before him; he knocked the five senses out of Dan O'Shaughran of Earrennamore, that herded many pigs by the sedgy banks of the Owen Erriff; he hollowed the left eye out of Larry Mulcahy, that lived on the Devil's Mother Mountain—never again did Larry set the two eyes of him on his high mountain-cradle; he killed Black Michael Joyce by a beautiful swooping blow on the side of the head—who would have dreamt that Black Michael had so thin a skull?

For near an hour Mat triumphed, then suddenly he went down under foot. At first he was missed only by those nearest him, and they took it for granted that he was up again and fighting. But when the Aughavanna men found themselves outnumbered and driven back to the Village, a great fear came on them, for they knew that all Ireland could not outnumber them if Mat was to the fore. Then disaster and rout took them, and they were forced backwards up the street, struggling desperately, till hardly a man of them could stand.

And when the victors were shouting themselves dumb, and drinking themselves blind, the beaten men looked for their leader. Long Mat was prone, his forehead was smashed, his face had been trampled into the mud—he had done with fighting. His death was untimely, yet he fell as he would have chosen— in a friendly battle. For when a man falls under the hand of an enemy (as of any one who differs from him in creed or politics), revenge and black blood live after him; but he who takes his death from the kindly hand of a friend leaves behind him no ill-will, but only gentle regret for the mishap.

When the dead had been duly waked for two days and nights, the burying day came. All the morning Long Mat Murnane's coffin lay on four chairs by his cabin, with a kneeling ring of disheveled women *keening* round it. Every soul in Aughavanna and their kith and kin had gathered to do him honor. And when the Angelus bell rang across the Valley from the chapel, the mourners fell into ranks, the coffin was lifted on the rough hearse, and the motley funeral—a line of carts with a mob of peasants behind, a few riding, but most of them on foot— moved slowly towards Carrala. The women were crying bitterly, *keening* like an Atlantic gale; the men looked as sober as if they had never heard of a wake, and spoke sadly of the dead man, and of what a pity it was that he could not see his funeral.

The Joyces too had waited, as was the custom, for the Angelus bell, and now Black Michael's funeral was moving slowly towards Carrala along the other side of the bog. Before long either party could hear the *keening* of the other, for you know the roads grow nearer as they converge on Carrala. Before long either party began to fear that the other would be there first.

There is no knowing how it happened, but the funerals began to go quicker, keeping abreast; then still quicker, till the women had to break into a trot to keep up; then still quicker, till the donkeys were galloping, and till every one raced at full speed, and the rival parties broke into a wild shout of "Augha-vanna *abu*!" "Meehul Dhu for ever!"

For the dead men were racing—feet foremost—to the grave; they were rivals even in death. Never did the world see such a race, never was there such whooping and shouting. Where the roads meet in Callanan's Field the hearses were abreast; neck to neck they dashed across the trampled fighting-place, while the coffins jogged and jolted as if the two dead men were struggling to get out and lead the rush; neck to neck they reached the churchyard, and the hearses jammed in the gate. Behind them the carts crashed into one another, and the mourners shouted as if they were mad.

But the quick wit of the Aughavanna men triumphed, for they seized their long coffin and dragged it in, and Long Mat Murnane won his last race. The shout they gave then deafened the echo up in the mountains, so that it has never been the same since. The victors wrung one another's hands; they hugged one another.

"Himself would be proud," they cried, "if he hadn't been dead!"

Some Parishioners

[GEORGE MOORE]

I

The way before Father Maguire was plain enough, yet his uncle's apathy and constitutional infirmity of purpose seemed at times to thwart him. Only two or three days ago, he had come running down from Kilmore with the news that a baby had been born out of wedlock, and what do you think? Father Stafford had shown no desire that his curate should denounce the girl from the altar.

"The greatest saints," he said, "have been kind, and have found excuses for the sins of others."

And a few days later, when he told his uncle that the Salvationists had come to Kilmore, and that he had walked up the village street and slit their drum with a carving-knife, his uncle had not approved of his conduct, and what had especially annoyed Father Tom was that his uncle seemed to deplore the slitting of the drum in the same way as he deplored that the Kavanaghs had a barrel of porter in every Saturday, as one of those regrettable excesses to which human nature is liable. On being pressed, he agreed with his nephew that dancing and drinking were no preparation for the Sabbath, but he would not agree that evil could be suppressed by force. He even hinted that too strict a rule brought about a revolt against the rule, and when Father Tom expressed his disbelief at any revolt against the authority of the priest, Father Stafford said:

"They may just leave you, they may just go to America."

"Then you think that it is our condemnation of sin that is driving the people to America."

"My dear Tom, you told me the other day that you met a boy and girl walking along the roadside, and drove them home. You told me you were sure they were talking about things they shouldn't talk about; you have no right to assume these things. You're asking of the people an abstinence you don't practise yourself. Sometimes your friends are women."

"Yes. But——"

Father Tom's anger prevented him from finding an adequate argument, and Father Stafford pushed the tobacco-bowl towards his nephew.

"You're not smoking, Tom."

"Your point is that a certain amount of vice is inherent in human nature, and that if we raise the standard of virtuous living our people will escape from us to New York or London."

"The sexes mix freely everywhere in Western Europe; only in Ireland and Turkey is there any attempt made to separate them."

Later in the evening Father Tom insisted that the measure of responsibility was always the same.

"I should be sorry," said his uncle, "to say that those who inherit drunkenness bear the same burden of responsibility as those who come of parents who are quite sane——"

"You cannot deny, uncle John, that free will and predestination——"

"My dear Tom, I really must go to bed. It is after midnight."

And as he walked home, Father Maguire thought of the great change he perceived in his uncle. He liked an hour's small-talk after dinner, his pipe, his glass of grog, his bed at eleven o'clock, and Father Maguire thought with sorrow of their great disputations, sometimes prolonged till after three o'clock. The passionate scholiast of Maynooth seemed to him unrecognizable in the esurient Vicar-General, only occasionally interested in theology, at certain hours and when he felt particularly well. The first seemed incompatible with the second, his mind not being sufficiently acute to see that after all no one can discuss theology for more than five and twenty years without wearying of the subject.

The moon was shining among the hills and the mystery of the landscape seemed to aggravate his sensibility, and he asked himself if the guardians of the people should not fling themselves into the forefront of the battle. If men came to preach heresy in his parish was he not justified in slitting their drum?

He had recourse to prayer, and he prayed for strength and for guidance. He had accepted the Church, and in the Church he saw only apathy, neglect, and bad administration on the part of his superiors . . . He had read that great virtues are, like large sums of money, deposited in the bank, whereas humility is like the pence, always at hand, always current. Obedience to our superiors is the sure path. He could not persuade himself that it was right for him to allow the Kavanaghs to continue a dissolute life of drinking and dancing. They were the talk of the parish; and he would have spoken against them from the altar, but his uncle had advised him not to do so. Perhaps his uncle was right; he might be right regarding the Kavanaghs. In the main he disagreed with his uncle, but in this particular instance it might be well to wait and pray that matters might improve.

Father Tom believed Ned Kavanagh to be a good boy. Ned was going to marry Mary Byrne, and Father Tom had made up this marriage. The Byrnes did not care for the marriage—they were prejudiced against Ned on account of his family. But he was not going to allow them to break off the marriage. He was sure of Ned, but in order to make quite sure he would get him to take the pledge. Next morning, when the priest had done his breakfast, the servant opened the door, and told him that Ned Kavanagh was outside, and wanted to see him.

It was a pleasure to look at this nice clean boy, with his winning smile, and the priest thought that Mary could not wish for a better husband. The priest had done his breakfast, and was about to open his newspaper, but he wanted to see Ned Kavanagh, and he told his servant to let him in. Ned's smile seemed a little fainter than usual, and his face was paler; the priest wondered, and presently Ned told the priest that he had come to confession, and, going down on his knees, he told the priest that he had been drunk last Saturday night, and that he had come to take the pledge. He would never do any good while he was at home, and one of the reasons he gave for wishing to marry Mary Byrne was his desire to leave home. The priest asked him if matters were mending, and if his sister showed any signs of wishing to be married.

"Sorra sign," said Ned.

"That's bad news you're bringing me," said the priest, and he walked up and down the room, and they talked over Kate's wilful character.

"From the beginning she didn't like living at home," said the priest.

"I wouldn't be caring about living at home," said Ned.

"But for a different reason," said the priest. "You want to leave home to get married, and have a wife and children, if God is pleased to give you children."

He sat thinking of the stories he had heard. He had heard that Kate had come back from her last situation in a cab, wrapped up in blankets, saying she was ill. On inquiry it was found that she had only been three or four days in her situation; three weeks had to be accounted for. He had questioned her himself regarding this interval, but had not been able to get any clear and definite answer from her.

"She and mother do be always quarrelling about Pat Connex."

"It appears," said the priest, "that your mother went out with a jug of porter under her apron, and offered a sup of it to Pat, who was talking with Peter M'Shane, and now he is up at your cabin every Saturday."

"That's so," said Ned.

"Mrs. Connex was here the other day, and I tell you that if Pat marries your sister he will find himself cut off with a shilling."

"She's been agin us all the while," said Ned. "Her money has made her proud, but I wouldn't be blaming her. If I had the fine house she has, maybe I would be as proud as she."

"Maybe you would," said the priest. "But what I'm thinking of is your sister Kate. She'll never get Pat Connex. Pat won't ever go against his mother."

"Well, you see he comes up and plays the melodeon on Saturday night," said Ned, "and she can't stop him from doing that."

"Then you think," said the priest, "that Pat will marry your sister?"

"I don't think she is thinking about him."

"If she doesn't want to marry him, what's all this talk about?"

"She does like to be meeting Pat in the evenings and to be walking out with him, and him putting his arm round her waist and kiss her, saving your reverence's presence."

"It is strange that you should be so unlike. You come here and ask me to speak to Mary Byrne's parents for you, and that I'll do, Ned, and it will be all right. You will make a good husband, and though you were drunk last night, you have taken the pledge to-day. And I will make a good marriage for Kate, too, if she'll listen to me."

"And who may your reverence be thinking of?"

"I'm thinking of Peter M'Shane. He gets as much

as six shillings a week and his keep on Murphy's farm, and his mother has got a bit of money, and they have a nice, clean cabin. Now listen to me. There is a poultry lecture at the schoolhouse to-night. Do you think you could bring your sister with you?"

"We did use to keep a great many hins at home, and Kate had the feeding of them, and now she's turned agin them, and she wants to live in town, and she even tells Pat Connex she would not marry a farmer, however much he was worth."

"But if you tell her that Pat Connex will be at the lecture, will she come?"

"Yes, your reverence, if she believes me."

"Then do as I bid you," said the priest; "you can tell her that Pat Connex will be there."

II

After leaving the priest Ned crossed over the road to avoid the public-house, and went for a walk on the hills. It was about five when he turned towards the village. On his way there he met his father, and Ned told him that he had been to see the priest, and that he was going to take Mary to the lecture.

"They're quarrelling at home."

Michael was very tired, and he thought it was pretty hard to come home after a long day's work to find his wife and daughter quarrelling.

"I am sorry your dinner isn't ready, father," said Kate, "but it won't be long now. I'll cut the bacon."

"I met Ned on the road," her father answered. "It's sorry I am that he has gone to fetch Mary. He's going to take her to the lecture on poultry-keeping at the schoolhouse."

"Ah, he has been to the priest, has he?" said Kate, and her mother asked her why she said that, and the wrangle began again.

Ned was the peacemaker; there was generally quiet in the cabin when he was there. And he dropped in as Michael was finishing his dinner, bringing with him Mary, a small, fair girl, who everybody said would keep his cabin tidy. His mother and sisters were broad-shouldered women with blue-black hair and red cheeks, and it was said that he had said he would like to bring a little fair hair in the family.

"We've just looked in for a minute," said Mary. "Ned said that perhaps you'd be coming with us."

"All the boys in the village will be there to-night," said Ned. "You had better come with us." And pretending he wanted to get a coal of fire to light his pipe, Ned whispered to Kate as he passed her, "Pat Connex will be there."

She looked at the striped sunshade she had brought back from the dressmaker's—she had once been apprenticed to a dressmaker—but Ned said that a storm was blowing and she had better leave the sunshade behind.

The rain beat in their faces and the wind came sweeping down the mountain and made them stagger. Sometimes the road went straight on, sometimes it turned suddenly and went uphill. After walking for a mile they came to the schoolhouse. A number of men were waiting outside, and one of the boys told them that the priest had said they were to keep a look-out for the lecturer, and Ned said that he had better stay with them, that his lantern would be useful to show her the way. The women had collected into one corner, and the priest was walking up and down a long, smoky room, his hands thrust into the pockets of his overcoat. Now he stopped in his walk to scold two children who were trying to light a peat fire in a tumble-down grate.

"Don't be tired, go on blowing," he said. "You are the laziest child I have seen this long while."

Ned came in and blew out his lantern, but the lady he had mistaken for the lecturer was a lady who had come to live in the neighbourhood lately, and the priest said:

"You must be very much interested in poultry, ma'am, to come out on such a night as this."

The lady stood shaking her waterproof.

"Now, then, Lizzie, run to your mother and get the lady a chair."

And when the child came back with the chair, and the lady was seated by the fire, he said:

"I'm thinking there will be no lecturer here tonight, and that it would be kind of you if you were to give the lecture yourself. You have read some books about poultry, I am sure?"

"Well, a little—but——"

"Oh, that doesn't matter," said the priest. "I'm sure the book you have read is full of instruction."

He walked up the room towards a group of men and told them they must cease talking, and coming back to the young woman he said:

"We shall be much obliged if you will say a few words about poultry. Just say what you have in your mind about the different breeds."

The young woman again protested, but the priest said:

"You will do it very nicely." And he spoke like one who is not accustomed to being disobeyed. "We will give the lecturer five minutes more."

"Is there no farmer's wife who could speak?" the young lady asked in a fluttering voice. "She'd know much more than I. I see Biddy M'Hale there. She has done very well with her poultry."

"I dare say she has," said the priest, "but the people would pay no attention to her. She is one of themselves. It would be no amusement to them to hear her."

The young lady asked if she might have five minutes to scribble a few notes. The priest said he would wait a few minutes, but it did not matter much what she said.

"But couldn't someone dance or sing?" said the young lady.

"Dancing and singing!" said the priest. "No!"

And the young lady hurriedly scribbled a few notes about fowls for laying, fowls for fattening, regular feeding, warm houses, and something about a percentage of mineral matter. She had not half finished when the priest said:

"Now will you stand over there near the harmonium. Whom shall I announce?"

The young woman told him her name, and he led her to the harmonium and left her talking, addressing most of her instruction to Biddy M'Hale, a long, thin, pale-faced woman, with wistful eyes.

"This won't do," said the priest, interrupting the lecturer—"I'm not speaking to you, miss, but to my people. I don't see one of you taking notes, not even you, Biddy M'Hale, though you have made a fortune out of your hins. Didn't I tell you from the pulpit that you were to bring pencil and paper and write down all you heard? If you had known years ago all this young lady is going to tell you, you would be rolling in your carriages to-day."

Then the priest asked the lecturer to go on, and

the lady explained that to get hens to lay about Christmas time, when eggs fetched the best price, you must bring on your pullets early.

"You must," she said, "set your eggs in January."

"You hear that," said the priest. "Is there anyone who has got anything to say about that? Why is it that you don't set your eggs in January?"

No one answered, and the lecturer went on to tell of the advantages that would come to the poultry-keeper whose eggs were hatched in December.

As she said this, the priest's eyes fell upon Biddy M'Hale, and, seeing that she was smiling, he asked her if there was any reason why eggs could not be hatched in the beginning of January.

"Now, Biddy, you must know all about this, and I insist on your telling us. We are here to learn."

Biddy did not answer.

"Then what were you smiling at?"

"I wasn't smiling, your reverence."

"Yes; I saw you smiling. Is it because you think there isn't a brooding hin in January?"

It had not occurred to the lecturer that hens might not be brooding so early in the year, and she waited anxiously. At last Biddy said:

"Well, your reverence, it isn't because there are no hins brooding. You'll get brooding hins at every time in the year; but, you see, you couldn't be rearing chickens earlier than March. The end of February is the earliest ever I saw. But, sure, if you could be rear-ing them in January, all that the young lady said would be quite right. I have nothing to say agin it. I have no fault to find with anything she says, your reverence."

"Only that it can't be done," said the priest. "Well, you ought to know, Biddy."

The villagers were laughing.

"That will do," said the priest. "I don't mind your having a bit of amusement, but you're here to learn."

And as he looked round the room, quieting the villagers into silence, his eyes fell on Kate. He looked for the others, and spied Pat Connex and Peter M'Shane near the door, "They're here, too," he thought. "When the lecture is over I will see them and bring them all together. Kate Kavanagh won't go home until she promises to marry Peter. I have had enough of her goings on in my parish."

But Kate had caught sight of Peter. She would get no walk home with Pat that night, and she suspected her brother of having done this for a purpose and got up to go.

"I don't want anyone to leave this room," said the priest. "Kate Kavanagh, why are you going? Sit down till the lecture is over."

And as Kate had not strength to defy the priest, she sat down, and the lecturer continued for a little while longer. The priest could see that the lecturer had said nearly all she had to say, and he had begun to wonder how the evening's amusement was to be prolonged. It would not do to let the people go home until Michael Dunne had closed his public-house, and the priest looked round the audience thinking which one he might call upon to say a few words on the subject of poultry-keeping.

From one of the back rows a voice was heard: "What about the pump, your reverence?"

"Well, indeed, you may ask," said the priest.

And immediately he began to speak of the wrong they had suffered by not having a pump in the village. The fact that Almighty God had endowed Kilmore with a hundred mountain streams did not release the authorities from the obligation of supplying the village with a pump. Had not the authorities put up one in the neighbouring village?

"You should come out," he said, "and fight for your rights. You should take off your coats like men, and if you do I'll see that you get your rights," and he looked round for someone to speak.

There was a landlord among the audience, and as he was a Catholic the priest called upon him to speak. He said that he agreed with the priest in the main. They should have their pump, if they wanted a pump; if they didn't, he would suggest that they asked for something else. Farmer Byrne said he did not want a pump, and then everyone spoke his mind, and things got mixed. The Catholic landlord regretted that Father Maguire was against allowing a poultry-yard to the patients in the lunatic asylum. If, instead of supplying a pump, the Government would sell them eggs for hatching at a low price, something might be gained. If the Government would not do this, the Government might be induced to supply books on poultry free of charge. It took the Catholic landlord half an hour to express his ideas regarding the asylum, the pump, and the duties of the Government, and in this way the priest succeeded in delaying the departure of the audience till after closing time. "However fast they walk," he said to himself, "they won't get to Michael Dunne's public-house in ten minutes, and he will be shut by then." It devolved upon him to bring the evening's amusement to a close with a few remarks, and he said:

"Now, the last words I have to say to you I'll address to the women. Now listen to me. If you pay more attention to your poultry you'll never be short of half a sovereign to lend your husbands, your sons, or your brothers."

These last words produced an approving shuffling of feet in one corner of the room, and seeing that nothing more was going to happen the villagers got up and they went out very slowly, the women curtseying and the men lifting their caps to the priest as they passed him.

He had signed to Ned and Mary that he wished to speak to them, and after he had spoken to Ned he called Kate and reminded her that he had not seen her at confession lately.

"Pat Connex and Peter M'Shane, now don't you be going. I will have a word with you presently."

And while Kate tried to find an excuse to account for her absence from confession, the priest called to Ned and Mary, who were talking at a little distance. He told them he would be waiting for them in church to-morrow, and he said he had never made a marriage that gave him more pleasure. He alluded to the fact that they had come to him. He was responsible for this match, and he accepted the responsibility gladly. His uncle, the Vicar-General, had delegated all the work of the parish to him.

"Father Stafford," he said abruptly, "will be very glad to hear of your marriage, Kate Kavanagh."

"My marriage," said Kate. . . . "I don't think I shall ever be married."

"Now, why do you say that?" said the priest.

Kate did not know why she had said that she would never be married. However, she had to give some reason, and she said:

"I don't think, your reverence, anyone would have me."

"You are not speaking your mind," said the priest,

a little sternly. "It is said that you don't want to be married, that you like courting better."

"I'd like to be married well enough."

"Those who wish to make safe, reliable marriages consult their parents and they consult the priest. I have made your brother's marriage for him. Why don't you come to me and ask me to make up a marriage for you?"

"I think a girl should make her own marriage, your reverence."

"And what way do you go about making up a marriage? Walking about the roads in the evening, and turning into public-houses, and leaving your situations. It seems to me, Kate Kavanagh, you have been a long time making up this marriage.

"Now, Pat Connex, I've got a word with you. You're a good boy, and I know you don't mean any harm by it; but I have been hearing tales about you. You've been up to Dublin with Kate Kavanagh. Your mother came up to speak to me about this matter yesterday, and she said: 'Not a penny of my money will he ever get if he marries her,' meaning the girl before you. Your mother said: 'I've got nothing to say against her, but I've got a right to choose my own daughter-in-law.' Those are your mother's very words, Pat, so you had better listen to reason. Do you hear me, Kate?"

"I hear your reverence."

"And if you hear me, what have you got to say to that?"

"He's free to go after the girl he chooses, your reverence," said Kate.

"There's been courting enough," the priest said. "If you aren't going to be married you must give up keeping company. I see Paddy Boyle outside the door. Go home with him. Do you hear what I'm saying, Pat? Go straight home, and no stopping about the roads. Just do as I bid you; go straight home to your mother."

Pat did not move at the bidding of the priest. He stood watching Kate as if he were waiting for a sign from her, but Kate did not look at him.

"Do you hear what I'm saying to you?" said the priest.

"Yes, I hear," said Pat.

"And aren't you going?" said the priest.

Everyone was afraid Pat would raise his hand against the priest, and they looked such strong men, both of them, that everyone wondered which would get the better of the other.

"You won't go home when I tell you to do so. We will see if I can't put you out of the door then."

"If you weren't a priest," said Pat, "the divil a bit of you would put me out of the door."

"If I weren't a priest I would break every bone in your body for talking to me like that. Now out you go," he said, taking him by the collar, and he put him out.

"And now, Kate Kavanagh," said the priest, coming back from the door, "you said you didn't marry because no man would have you. Peter has been waiting for you ever since you were a girl of sixteen years old, and I may say it for him, since he doesn't say much himself, that you have nearly broken his heart."

"I'm sure I never meant it. I like Pether."

"You acted out of recklessness without knowing what you were doing."

A continual smile floated round Peter's moustache, and he looked like a man to whom rebuffs made no difference. His eyes were patient and docile; and whether it was the presence of this great and true love by her side, or whether it was the presence of the priest, Kate did not know, but a great change came over her, and she said:

"I know that Pether has been very good, that he has a liking for me. . . . If he wishes to put the ring on me——"

When Kate gave him her hand there was a mist in his eyes, and he stood trembling before her.

The Gombeen Man

❧

[**BRAM STOKER**]

In the midst of the buzz of conversation the clattering of hoofs was heard. There was a shout, and the door opened again and admitted a stalwart stranger of some fifty years of age, with a strong, determined face, with kindly eyes, well-dressed, but wringing wet and haggard, and seemingly disturbed in mind. One arm hung useless by his side.

"Here's one of them!" said Father Peter.

"God save all here," said the man as he entered.

Room was made for him at the fire. He no sooner came near it and tasted the heat than a cloud of steam arose from him.

"Man! but ye're wet," said Mrs. Kelligan. "One'd think ye'd been in the lake beyant!"

"So I have," he answered, "worse luck! I rid all the way from Galway this blessed day to be here in time, but the mare slipped coming down Curragh Hill, and threw me over the bank into the lake. I wor in the wather nigh three hours before I could get out, for I was forninst the Curragh Rock, an' only got a foothold in a chink, an' had to hold on wid me one arm, for I fear the other is broke."

"Dear! dear! dear!" interrupted the woman. "Sthrip yer coat off, acushla, an' let us see if we can do anythin'."

He shook his head as he answered:

"Not now; there's not a minute to spare. I must get up the Hill at once. I should have been there be six o'clock. But mayn't be too late yit. The mare has broke down entirely. Can any one here lend me a horse?"

There was no answer till Andy spoke:

"Me mare is in the shtable, but this gintleman has me'an her for the day, an' I have to lave him at Carnaclif tonight."

Here I struck in:

"Never mind me, Andy. If you can help this gentleman, do so. I'm better off here than driving through the storm. He wouldn't want to go on with a broken arm if he hadn't good reason."

The man looked at me with grateful eagerness.

"Thank yer honor kindly. It's a rale gintleman ye are! An' I hope ye'll never be sorry for helpin' a poor fellow in sore trouble."

"What's wrong, Phelim?" asked the priest. "Is there anything troubling you that any one here can get rid of?"

"Nothin', Father Pether, thank ye kindly. The trouble is me own intirely, an' no wan here could help me. But I must see Murdock to-night."

There was a general sigh of commiseration; all understood the situation.

"Musha!" said old Dan Moriarty, *sotto voce.* "An' is that the way of it? An' is he, too, in the clutches iv that wolf—him that we all thought was so warrum? Glory be to God! but it 's a quare wurrld, it is; an' it 's few there is in it that is what they seems. Me poor frind, is there any way I can help ye? I have a bit iv money by me that yer wilkim to the lend iv av ye want it."

The other shook his head gratefully.

"Thank ye kindly, Dan, but I have the money all right; it 's only the time I 'm in trouble about!"

"Only the time, me poor chap! It's be time that the divil helps Black Murdock an' the likes iv him, the most iv all! God be good to ye if he has got his clutch on yer back, an' has time on his side, for ye 'll want it!"

"Well, anyhow, I must be goin' now. Thank ye kindly, neighbors all. When a man 's in throuble, sure the goodwill of his frinds is the greatest comfort ye can have."

"All but one, remember that—all but one!" said the priest.

"Thank ye kindly, Father, I shan't forget. Thank ye, Andy, an' you, too, young sir; I 'm much beholden to ye. I hope some day I may have it to do a good turn for ye in return. Thank ye kindly again, and good-night." He shook my hand warmly, and was going to the door, when old Dan said:

"An' as for that black-jawed ruffian, Murdock—" He paused, for the door suddenly opened, and a harsh voice said:

"Murtagh Murdock is here to answer for himself!" It was my man at the window.

There was a sort of paralyzed silence in the room, through which came the whisper of one of the old women:

"Musha! talk iv the divil!"

Joyce's face grew very white; one hand instinctively grasped his riding-switch, the other hung uselessly by his side. Murdock spoke:

"I kem here expectin' to meet Phelim Joyce. I thought I 'd save him the throuble of comin' wid the money." Joyce said in a husky voice:

"What do ye mane? I have the money right enough here. I 'm sorry I 'm a bit late, but I had a bad accident—bruk me arrum, an' was nigh dhrownded in the Curragh Lake. But I was goin' up to ye at once, bad as I am, to pay ye yer money, Murdock." The Gombeen Man interrupted him:

"But it isn't to me ye 'd have to come, me good

man. Sure, it 's the sheriff himself that was waitin' for ye', an' whin ye didn't come"—here Joyce winced; the speaker smiled—"he done his work."

"What wurrk, acushla?" asked one of the women. Murdock answered, slowly:

"He sould the lease iv the farrum known as the Shleenanaher in open sale, in accordance wid the terrums of his notice, duly posted, and wid warnin' given to the houldher iv the lease."

There was a long pause. Joyce was the first to speak:

"Ye're jokin', Murdock. For God's sake, say ye 're jokin'! Ye tould me yerself that I might have time to git the money. An' ye tould me that the puttin' me farrum up for sale was only a matther iv forrum to let me pay ye back in me own way. Nay, more, ye asked me not to tell any iv the neighbors, for fear some iv them might want to buy some iv me land. An' it 's niver so, that whin ye got me aff to Galway to rise the money, ye went on wid the sale, behind me back—wid not a soul by to spake for me or mine—an' sould up all I have! No, Murtagh Murdock, ye 're a hard man, I know, but ye wouldn't do that! Ye wouldn't do that!"

Murdock made no direct reply to him, but said, seemingly to the company generally:

"I ixpected to see Phelim Joyce at the sale to-day, but as I had some business in which he was consarned,

I kem here where I knew there'd be neighbors—an', sure, so there is."

He took out his pocket-book and wrote names: "Father Pether Ryan, Daniel Moriarty, Bartholomew Moynahan, Andhrew McGlown, Mrs. Katty Kelligan—that's enough! I want ye all to see what I done. There 's nothin' undherhand about me! Phelim Joyce, I give ye formil notice that yer land was sould an' bought be me, for ye broke yer word to repay me the money lint ye before the time fixed. Here 's the sheriff's assignment, an' I tell ye before all these witnesses that I 'll proceed with ejectment on title at wanst."

All in the room were as still as statues. Joyce was fearfully still and pale, but when Murdock spoke the word "ejectment" he seemed to wake in a moment to frenzied life. The blood flushed up in his face, and he seemed about to do something rash; but with a great effort he controlled himself and said:

"Mr. Murdock, ye won't be too hard. I got the money to-day—it 's here—but I had an accident that delayed me. I was thrown into Curragh Lake and nigh dhrownded, an' me arrum is bruk. Don't be so close as an hour or two; ye'll never be sorry for it. I 'll pay ye all, and more, and thank ye into the bargain all me life. Ye 'll take back the paper, won't ye, for me children's sake—for Norah's sake?"

He faltered; the other answered with an evil smile:

"Phelim Joyce, I 've waited years for this moment. Don't ye know me betther nor to think I would go back on meself whin I have shtarted on a road? I wouldn't take yer money, not if every pound note was spread into an acre and cut up in tin-pound notes. I want yer land—I have waited for it, an' I mane to have it! Now don't beg me any more, for I won't go back; an' tho' it 's many a grudge I owe ye, I square them all before the neighbors be refusin' yer prayer. The land is mine, bought be open sale; an' all the judges an' coorts in Ireland can't take it from me! An' what do ye say to that now, Phelim Joyce?"

The tortured man had been clutching the ash sapling which he had used as a riding-whip, and from the nervous twitching of his fingers I knew that something was coming. And it came; for, without a word, he struck the evil face before him— struck as quick as a flash of lightning—such a blow that the blood seemed to leap out round the stick, and a vivid welt rose in an instant. With a wild, savage cry the Gombeen Man jumped at him; but there were others in the room as quick, and before another blow could be struck on either side both men were grasped by strong hands and held back.

Murdock's rage was tragic. He yelled, like a wild beast, to be let get at his opponent. He cursed and blasphemed so outrageously that all were silent, and only the stern voice of the priest was heard:

"Be silent, Murtagh Murdock! Aren't you afraid that the God overhead will strike you dead? With such a storm as is raging as a sign of his power, you are a foolish man to tempt him."

The man stopped suddenly, and stern, dogged sullenness took the place of his passion. The priest went on:

"As for you, Phelim Joyce, you ought to be ashamed of yourself. Ye're not one of my people, but I speak as your own clergyman would if he were here. Only this day has the Lord seen fit to spare you from a terrible death; and yet you dare to go back of his mercy with your angry passion. You had cause for anger—or temptation to it, I know—but you must learn to kiss the chastening rod, not spurn it. The Lord knows what he is doing for you as for others, and it may be that you will look back on this day in gratitude for his doing, and in shame for your own anger. Men, hold off your hands—let those two men go; they'll quarrel no more—before me at any rate, I hope."

The men drew back. Joyce held his head down, and a more despairing figure or a sadder one I never saw. He turned slowly away, and, leaning against the wall, put his face between his hands and sobbed. Murdock scowled, and the scowl gave place to an evil smile as, looking all around, he said:

"Well, now that me work is done, I must be gettin' home."

"An' get some one to iron that mark out iv yer face," said Dan. Murdock turned again, and glared around him savagely as he hissed out:

"There 'll be iron for some one before I 'm done— mark me well! I 've never gone back or wakened yit whin I promised to have me own turn. There 's thim here what 'll rue this day yit! If I am the Shnake on the Hill—thin beware the Shnake. An' for him what shtruck me, he 'll be in bitther sorra for it yit—him an' his!" He turned his back and went to the door.

"Stop," said the priest. "Murtagh Murdock, I have a word to say to you—a solemn word of warning. Ye have to-day acted the part of Ahab towards Naboth the Jezreelite; beware of his fate! You have coveted your neighbor's goods; you have used your power without mercy; you have made the law an engine of oppression. Mark me! It was said of old that what measure men meted should be meted out to them again. God is very just. 'Be not deceived, God is not mocked. For what things a man shall sow, those also shall he reap.' Ye have sowed the wind this day; beware lest you reap the whirlwind! Even as God visited his sin upon Ahab the Samarian, and as he has visited similar sins on others in his own way, so shall he visit yours on you. You are worse than the land-grabber—worse than the man who only covets. Saintough is a virtue compared with your act. Remember the story of Naboth's vineyard, and the dreadful end of it. Don't answer me! Go and repent if you can, and leave sorrow and misery to be comforted by others, unless you wish to undo your wrong yourself. If you don't, then remember the curse that may come upon you yet!"

Without a word Murdock opened the door and went out, and a little later we heard the clattering of his horse's feet on the rocky road to Schleenanaher.

When it was apparent to all that he was really gone, a torrent of commiseration, sympathy, and pity broke over Joyce. The Irish nature is essentially emotional, and a more genuine and stronger feeling I never saw. Not a few had tears in their eyes, and one and all were manifestly deeply touched. The least moved was, to all appearance, poor Joyce himself. He seemed to have pulled himself together, and his sterling manhood and courage and pride stood by him. He seemed, however, to yield to the kindly wishes of his friends, and when we suggested that his hurt should be looked to he acquiesced:

"Yes, if you will. Betther not go home to poor Norah and distress her with it. Poor child! she'll have enough to bear without that."

His coat was taken off, and between us we managed to bandage the wound. The priest, who had some surgical knowledge, came to the conclusion that there was only a simple fracture. He splinted and bandaged the arm, and we all agreed that it would be better for Joyce to wait until the storm was over before starting for home. Andy said he could take him on the car, as he knew the road well, and that as it was partly on the road to Carnacliff, we should only have to make a short detour and would pass the house of the doctor, by whom the arm could be properly attended to.

So we sat around the fire again, while without the storm howled, and the fierce gusts which swept the valley seemed at times as if they would break in the door, lift off the roof, or in some way annihilate the time-worn cabin which gave us shelter.

There could, of course, be only one subject of conversation now, and old Dan simply interpreted the public wish when he said:

"Tell us, Phelim—sure, we 're all friends here— how Black Murdock got ye in his clutches? Sure, any wan of us would get you out of thim if he could."

There was a general acquiescence. Joyce yielded himself, and said:

"Let me thank ye, neighbors all, for yer kindness to me and mine this sorraful night. Well, I 'll say no more about that; but I 'll tell ye how it was that Murdock got me into his power. Ye know that boy of mine—Eugene?"

"Oh, and he 's the fine lad, God bless him! an' the good lad, too!"—this from the women.

"Well, ye know, too, that he got on so well whin I sint him to school that Dr. Walsh recommended me to make an ingineer of him. He said he had such promise that it was a pity not to see him get the right start in life, and he gave me, himself, a let-ther to Sir George Henshaw, the great ingineer. I wint and seen him, and he said he would take the boy. He tould me that there was a big fee to be paid, but I was not to throuble about that; at any rate, that he himself didn't want any fee, and he would ask his partner if he would give up his share too. But the latther was hard up for money. He said he couldn't give up all the fee, but that he would take half the fee, provided it was paid down in dhry money. Well, the regular fee to the firm was five hundhred pounds, and as Sir George had giv up half, an' only half, th' other half was to be paid, if that was possible. I hadn't got more 'n a few pounds by me; for what wid dhrainin' and plantin' and fencin', and the payin' the boy's schoolin' and the girl's at the Nuns' in Galway, it had put me to the pin iv me collar to find the money up to now. But I didn't like to let the boy lose his chance in life for want of an effort, an' I put me pride in me pocket an' kem an' asked Murdock for the money. He was very smooth an' nice wid me—I know why now—an' promised he would give it at wanst if I would give him security on me land. Sure, he joked an' laughed wid me, an' was that cheerful that I didn't misthrust him. He tould me it was

only forrums I was signin' that 'd never be used."
Here Dan Moriarty interrupted him:

"What did ye sign, Phelim?"

"There wor two papers. Wan was a writin' iv
some kind, that in considheration iv the money lent
an' his own land—which I was to take over if the
money wasn't paid at the time appointed—he was to
get me lease from me; an' the other was a power of
attorney to Enther Judgment for the amount if the
money wasn't paid at the right time. I thought I was
all safe, as I could repay him in the time named, an' if
the worst kem to the worst I might borry the money
from some wan else—for the lease is worth the sum
tin times over—an' repay him. Well, what's the use
of lookin' back, anyhow? I signed the papers—that
was a year ago an' one week. An' a week ago the
time was up!" He gulped down a sob, and went on:

"Well, ye all know the year gone has been a terrible
bad wan, an' as for me it was all I could do to hould
on—to make up the money was impossible. Thrue,
the lad cost me next to nothin', for he arned his keep
be exthra work, an' the girl, Norah, kem home from
school and labored wid me, an' we saved every penny
we could. But it was all no use; we couldn't get the
money together anyhow. Thin we had the misfortin
wid the cattle that ye all know of; an' three horses that
I sould in Dublin up an' died before the time I guar-
anteed them free from sickness." Here Andy struck in:

"Thrue for ye! Sure, there was some dhreadful dis-ordher in Dublin among the horse cattle, intirely; an' even Misther Docther Perfesshinal Ferguson himself couldn't git undher it!" Joyce went on:

"An' as the time grew nigh I began to fear, but Murdock came down to see me whin I was alone, an' tould me not to throuble about the money, an' not to mind about the sheriff, for he had to give him notice. 'An',' says he, 'I wouldn't, if I was you, tell Norah anythin' about it, for it might frighten the girl; for weemin is apt to take to heart things like that that 's only small things to min like us.' An' so, God forgive me, I believed him; an' I niver tould me child any-thing about it—even whin I got the notice from the sheriff. An' whin the notice tellin' iv the sale was posted up on me land, I tuk it down meself, so that the poor girl wouldn't be frightened—God help me!" He broke down for a bit, but then went on:

"But somehow I wasn't asy in me mind, an' whin the time iv the sale dhrew nigh I couldn't keep it to meself any longer, an' I tould Norah. That was only yisterday, and look at me to-day! Norah agreed wid me that we shouldn't trust the Gombeen, an' she sent me off to the Galway Bank to borry the money. She said I was an honest man an' farmed me own land, and that the bank might lind the money on it. An', sure enough, whin I wint there this mornin' be appointment, wid the Coadjuthor himself to inthroduce me, though he didn't know why I wanted the money—that was Norah's idea, and the Mother Superior settled it for her—the manager, who is a nice gintleman, tould me at wanst that I might have the money on me own note iv hand. I only gave him a formal writin', and I took away the money. Here it is in me pocket in good notes; they 're we wid the lake, but, I 'm thankful to say, all safe. But it 's too late, God help me!" Here he broke down for a minute, but recovered himself with an effort:

"Anyhow, the bank that thrusted me mustn't be wronged. Back the money goes to Galway as soon as iver I can get it there. If I am a ruined man, I needn't be a dishonest wan! But poor Norah! God help her! it will break her poor heart."

There was a spell of silence, only broken by sympathetic moans. The first to speak was the priest:

"Phelim Joyce, I told you a while ago, in the midst of your passion, that God knows what he is doin', and works in his own way. You 're an honest man, Phelim, and God knows it, and, mark me, he won't let you nor yours suffer. 'I have been young,' said the Psalmist, 'and now am old; and I have not seen the just forsaken, nor his seed seeking bread.' Think of that, Phelim; may it comfort you and poor Norah. God bless her, but she 's the good girl! You have much to be thankful for, with a daughter like her to comfort you at home and take the place of her poor mother, who was the best of women; and with such a boy as Eugene, winnin' name and credit, and perhaps fame to come, even in England itself. Thank God for his many mercies, Phelim, and trust him!"

There was a dead silence in the room. The stern man rose, and coming over took the priest's hand.

"God bless ye, Father!" he said, "it 's the true comforter ye are."

The scene was a most touching one; I shall never forget it. The worst of the poor man's trouble seemed now past. He had faced the darkest hour; he had told his trouble, and was now prepared to make the best of everything—for the time at least—for I could not reconcile to my mind the idea that that proud, stern man, would not take the blow to heart for many a long day, that it might even embitter his life.

The Wonderful Tune

[T. CROFTON CROKER]

Maurice Connor was the king, and that's no small word, of all the pipers in Munster. He could play jig and planxty without end, and Ollistrum's March, and the Eagle's Whistle, and the Hen's Concert, and odd tunes of every sort and kind. But he knew one, far more surprising than the rest, which had in it the power to set every thing dead or alive dancing.

In what way he learned it is beyond my knowledge, for he was mighty cautious about telling how he came by so wonderful a tune. At the very first note of that tune, the brogues began shaking upon the feet of all who heard it—old or young it mattered not—just as if their brogues had the ague; then the feet began going—going—going from under them, and at last up and away with them, dancing like mad!—whisking here, there, and every where, like a straw in a storm—there was no halting while the music lasted!

Not a fair, nor a wedding, nor a patron in the seven parishes round, was counted worth the speaking of without "blind Maurice and his pipes." His mother, poor woman, used to lead him about from one place to another, just like a dog.

Down through Iveragh—a place that ought to be proud of itself, for 'tis Daniel O'Connell's country—Maurice Connor and his mother were taking their rounds. Beyond all other places Iveragh is the place for stormy coast and steep mountains: as proper a spot it is as any in Ireland to get yourself drowned, or your neck broken on the land, should you prefer that. But, notwithstanding, in Ballinskellig bay there is a neat bit of ground, well fitted for diversion, and down from it towards the water, is a clean smooth piece of strand—the dead image of a calm summer's sea on a moonlight night, with just the curl of the small waves upon it.

Here it was that Maurice's music had brought from all parts a great gathering of the young men and the young women—O *the darlints!*—for 'twas not every day the strand of Trafraska was stirred up by the voice of a bagpipe. The dance began; and as pretty a rinkafadda it was as ever was danced. "Brave music," said every body, "and well done," when Maurice stopped.

"More power to your elbow, Maurice, and a fair wind in the bellows," cried Paddy Dorman, a hump-backed dancing-master, who was there to keep order. "'Tis a pity," said he, "if we'd let the piper run dry after such music; 'twould be a disgrace to Iveragh, that didn't come on it since the week of the three Sundays." So, as well became him, for he was always a decent man, says he: "Did you drink, piper?"

"I will, sir," says Maurice, answering the question on the safe side, for you never yet knew piper or schoolmaster who refused his drink.

"What will you drink, Maurice?" says Paddy.

"I'm no ways particular," says Maurice; "I drink any thing, and give God thanks, barring *raw* water; but if 'tis all the same to you, mister Dorman, maybe you wouldn't lend me the loan of a glass of whiskey."

"I've no glass, Maurice," said Paddy; "I've only the bottle."

"Let that be no hindrance," answered Maurice; "my mouth just holds a glass to the drop; often I've tried it, sure."

So Paddy Dorman trusted him with the bottle— more fool was he; and, to his cost, he found that though Maurice's mouth might not hold more than the glass at one time, yet, owing to the hole in his throat, it took many a filling.

"That was no bad whisky neither," says Maurice, handing back the empty bottle.

"By the holy frost, then!" says Paddy, "'tis but *cowld* comfort there's in that bottle now; and 'tis your word we must take for the strength of the whisky, for you've left us no sample to judge by:" and to be sure Maurice had not.

Now I need not tell any gentleman or lady with common understanding, that if he or she was to drink an honest bottle of whiskey at one pull, it is not at all the same thing as drinking a bottle of water; and in the whole course of my life, I never knew more than five men who could do so without being overtaken by the liquor. Of these Maurice Connor was not one, though he had a stiff head enough of his own—he was fairly tipsy. Don't think I blame him for it; 'tis often a good man's case; but true is the word that says, "when liquor's in, sense is out;" and puff, at a breath, before you could say "Lord save us!" out he blasted his wonderful tune.

'Twas really then beyond all belief or telling the dancing Maurice himself could not keep quiet; staggering now on one leg, now on the other, and rolling about like a ship in a cross sea, trying to humour the tune. There was his mother too, moving her old bones as light as the youngest girl of them all; but her dancing, no, nor the dancing of all the rest, is not worthy the speaking about to the work that was going on down on the strand. Every inch of it covered with all manner of fish jumping and plunging about to the music, and every moment more and more would tumble in out of the water, charmed by the wonderful tune. Crabs of monstrous size spun round and round on one claw with the nimbleness of a dancing-master, and twirled and tossed their other claws about like limbs that did not belong to them. It was a sight surprising to behold.

Never was such an ullabulloo in this world, before or since; 'twas as if heaven and earth were coming together; and all out of Maurice Connor's wonderful tune!

In the height of all these doings, what should there be dancing among the outlandish set of fishes but a beautiful young woman—as beautiful as the dawn of day! She had a cocked hat upon her head; from under it her long green hair—just the colour of the sea—fell down behind, without hinderance to her dancing. Her teeth were like rows of pearl; her lips for all the world looked like red coral; and she had an elegant gown, as white as the foam of the wave, with little rows of purple and red sea-weeds settled out upon it; for you never yet saw a lady, under the water or over the water, who had not a good notion of dressing herself out.

Up she danced at last to Maurice, who was flinging his feet from under him as fast as hops—for nothing in this world could keep still while that tune of his was going on—and says she to him, chaunting it out with a voice as sweet as honey—

> "I'm a lady of honour
> Who live in the sea
> Come down, Maurice Connor,
> And be married to me.

> "Silver plates and gold dishes
> You shall have, and shall be
> The king of the fishes,
> When you're married to me."

Drink was strong in Maurice's head, and out he chaunted in return for her great civility. It is not every lady, may be, that would be after making such an offer to a blind piper; therefore 'twas only right in him to give her as good as she gave herself—so says Maurice,

> "I'm obliged to you, madam:
> Off a gold dish or plate,
> If a king, and I had 'em,
> I could dine in great state.

> "With your own father's daughter
> I'd be sure to agree;

But to drink the salt water
Wouldn't do so with me!"

The lady looked at him quite amazed, and swinging her head from side to side like a great scholar, "Well," says she, "Maurice, if you're not a poet, where is poetry to be found?"

In this way they kept on at it, framing high compliments; one answering the other, and their feet going with the music as fast as their tongues. All the fish kept dancing too: Maurice heard the clatter, and was afraid to stop playing lest it might be displeasing to the fish, and not knowing what so many of them may take it into their heads to do to him if they got vexed.

Well, the lady with the green hair kept on coaxing of Maurice with soft speeches, till at last she over-persuaded him to promise to marry her, and be king over the fishes, great and small. Maurice was well fitted to be their king, if they wanted one that could make them dance; and he surely would drink, barring the salt water, with any fish of them all.

When Maurice's mother saw him, with that unnatural thing in the form of a green-haired lady as his guide, and he and she dancing down together so lovingly to the water's edge through the thick of the fishes, she called out after him to stop and come back. "Oh then," says she, "as if I was not widow enough before, there he is going away from me to be married to that scaly woman. And who knows but 'tis grandmother I may be to a hake or a cod—Lord help and pity me, but 'tis a mighty unnatural thing!—and maybe 'tis boiling and eating my own grandchild I'll be, with a bit of salt butter, and I not knowing it!— Oh Maurice, Maurice, if there's any love or nature left in you, come back to your own *ould* mother, who reared you like a decent Christian!"

Then the poor woman began to cry and ullagoane so finely that it would do any one good to hear her.

Maurice was not long getting to the rim of the water; there he kept playing and dancing on as if nothing was the matter, and a great thundering wave coming in towards him ready to swallow him up alive; but as he could not see it, he did not fear it. His mother it was who saw it plainly through the big tears that were rolling down her cheeks; and though she saw it, and her heart was aching as much as ever mother's heart ached for a son, she kept dancing, dancing, all the time for the bare life of her. Certain it was she could not help it, for Maurice never stopped playing that wonderful tune of his.

He only turned the bothered ear to the sound of his mother's voice, fearing it might put him out in his steps, and all the answer he made back was—

"Whisht with you, mother—sure I'm going to be king over the fishes down in the sea, and for a token of luck, and a sign that I am alive and well, I'll send you in, every twelvemonth on this day, a piece of burned wood to Trafraska." Maurice had not the power to say a word more, for the strange lady with the green hair, seeing the wave just upon them, covered him up with herself in a thing like a cloak with a big hood to it, and the wave curling over twice as high as their heads, burst upon the strand, with a rush and a roar that might be heard as far as Cape Clear.

That day twelvemonth the piece of burned wood came ashore in Trafraska. It was a queer thing for Maurice to think of sending all the way from the bottom of the sea. A gown or a pair of shoes would have been something like a present for his poor mother; but he had said it, and he kept his word. The bit of burned wood regularly came ashore on the appointed day for as good, ay, and better than a hundred years. The day is now forgotten, and maybe that is the reason why people say how Maurice Connor has stopped sending the luck-token to his mother. Poor woman, she did not live to get as much as one of them; for what through the loss of Maurice, and the fear of eating her own grandchildren, she died in three weeks after the dance—some say it was the fatigue that killed her, but whichever it was, Mrs. Connor was decently buried with her own people.

Seafaring men have often heard off the coast of Kerry, on a still night, the sound of music coming up from the water; and some, who have had good ears, could plainly distinguish Maurice Connor's voice singing these words to his pipes:—

Beautiful shore, with thy spreading strand,
Thy crystal water, and diamond sand;
Never would I have parted from thee
But for the sake of my fair ladie.

The Irishman Abroad

[GEORGE A. BIRMINGHAM]

The Irish who went to America during the last half of the nineteenth century left their homes with a sense in them of burning wrong. They were men who hated. They hated England and all in Irish life which stood for England. This hate bound them together. Irish political struggles, whether of the Fenian or the Parnell type, appealed to them. Ireland was, in one way or the other, up against England. But all this has changed. Irish politicians are no longer engaged in a struggle with England. They are in alliance with one set of Englishmen, and only against another set of Englishmen. There is in Irish politics at home an appeal to the man of party feeling. He is keen enough for his own party, keen enough against the other party, but when he gets to America neither of the parties at home can move him to any special enthusiasm. He no longer, when at home, hates England. He hates, if hate is not too strong a word, some Englishmen. There is a great difference between hating England and hating some Englishmen, when you are so far away that all Englishmen get blurred.

I do not mean to suggest that the sense of nationality has passed away from Ireland. It has not. In some ways the spirit of nationality is stronger in Ireland to-day than it was at any time during the last century. It has certainly penetrated to classes which used to have no consciousness of nationality at all. There are fewer Irishmen now who are ashamed of being Irish. There are more men now than ever, in every class, who want the good of Ireland as distinguished from that of England, or of any other country. But the sense of nationality has to a very large extent passed out of Irish political life. The platform appeal of the politician to the voter in Ireland now is far oftener an appeal to Irishmen as part of the British democracy, than to Irishmen as members of a nation governed against its will by foreigners. The ideas of John O'Leary, even the ideas of Parnell, have almost vanished from Irish political life. Instead of them we have the idea of international democracy.

This change of feeling in Ireland itself will make for a modification of the position of the Irish in

America. They will tend, as the older generation passes, to become more American and less Irish. This is already felt in Ireland itself. Of late years there has arisen a strong feeling against emigration. It is realised, as it used not to be, that Ireland loses those who go. The feeling is quite new. The phrase, "a greater Ireland beyond the seas," is beginning to mean a little less than it did, and the general consciousness of patriotic Irishmen at home is instinctively recognising this. But it is noticeable that the dislike of emigration has not found expression among politicians. The movement is outside politics. The local political boss is frequently an emigration agent and feels no inconsistency in his position.

It would be quite easy to exaggerate the present value of the change I have tried to indicate. The old solidarity of the Irish in America remains a fact. It is to Irish friends and relatives that our emigrants go. It is among Irish people that they live when they settle in America. It is Irish people whom they marry. But the tendency is towards a breaking away from this national isolation.

The movement against emigration at home has much in it besides the instinctive protest of a nation against the loss of its people. It is in part religious, and rests on a fear that faith is more easily lost in America than in Ireland. It is in part, no doubt, the result of shrinking of sensitive and loving souls from the horror of the great sorrow of farewell.

All emotions lose their keenness with repetition. The fine rapture of a joy is never quite so delightful as it was when the joy came first and was strange. The bitterness of sorrow and disappointment gradually loses its intensity when sorrow and disappointment become familiar things. Even insults cease after a while to move us to fierce anger. The law is universal; but there are some emotions which are only very slowly dulled. The sadness which comes of watching the departure of a trainful of Irish emigrants is one of these. We are, or ought to be, well accustomed to the sight. Those of us who have lived long in the country parts of Ireland have seen these trains, and travelled a little way in them many times; but we are still saddened, hardly less saddened, than when we saw them first.

There is one day in the week on which emigrants go, and in the west of Ireland one train on that day by which they travel. It goes slowly, stopping at every station, no matter how small, and at every station there is the same scene. The platform is crowded long before the train comes in. There are many old women weeping without restraint, mothers these, or grandmothers of the boys and girls who are going. Their eyes are swollen. Their cheeks are tear-stained. Every now and then one of them wails aloud, and the others, catching at the sound, wail with her, their voices rising and falling in a kind of weird melody, like the ancient plain-song of the Church. There are men too, but they are more silent. Very often their eyes are wet. Their lips, tightly pressed, twitch spasmodically. Occasionally an uncontrollable sob breaks from one of them. The boys and girls who are to go are helplessly sorrow-stricken. It is no longer possible for them to weep, for they have wept too much already. They are drooping despairingly. At their feet are carpet-bags and little yellow tin trunks, each bearing a great flaring steamboat label. They wear stiff new clothes; shoddy tweed suits from the shop of the village draper, dresses and blouses long discussed with some country dressmaker. These pitiful braveries mark them out unmistakably from the men in muddy frieze and the women in wide crimson petticoats, with shawls over their heads, who have come to say good-bye.

The train comes in. There is a rush to the carriage doors. Soon the windows of the carriages are filled with tear-stained faces. Hands are stretched out, grasped, held tight. Final kisses are pressed on lips and cheeks. The guard of the train gives his signal at last. The engine whistles. A porter, mercifully brutal, by main force pushes the people back. The train moves slowly, gathers speed. For a while the crowd moves along the platform beside the train. Then a long, sad cry rises, swelling to a pitch of actual agony. Some brave soul somewhere chokes down a sob, waves his hat, and makes a pretence to cheer. Then the scene is over.

What happens next in the railway carriages? For a while there is sobbing or silence. Then wonder and the excitement of change begin to take the place of grief. Words are whispered, questions asked. Little stores of money are taken out and counted over. Steamboat tickets are examined, unfolded, folded, put in yet securer places. Already the present is something more than a dull ache; and the future is looked to as well as the past.

What happens next to the crowd which was left behind? In little groups the men and women go slowly back along the country roads to the houses left at dawn, go back to take up the work of every day. Poverty is a merciful mistress to those whom she holds in bondage. There are fields to be dug, the cattle to be tended, the bread to be made. The steady succession of things which must be done dulls the edge of grief. They suffer less who are obliged to work as well as weep. But the sorrow remains. He has but a shallow knowledge of our people who supposes that because they go about the business of their lives afterwards as they did before there is no lasting reality in their grief. An Irish mother will say: "I had seven childer, but there's only two of them left to me now. I buried two and three is in America." She classes those who have crossed the sea with those who are dead. Both are lost to her.

Sometimes those who have gone are indeed lost utterly. There comes a letter once, and, after a long interval, another letter. Then no more letters nor any news at all. More often there is some kind of touch kept with the people at home. Letters come at Christmas time, often with very welcome gifts of money in them. There are photographs. Molly, whom we all knew when she was a bare-footed child running home from school, whom we remember as a half-grown girl climbing into her father's cart on market-days, appears almost as a stranger in her picture. Her clothes are grand beyond our imaginings. Her face has a new look in it. There are few Irish country houses in which such photographs are not shown with a mixture of pride and grief. It is a fine thing that Molly is so grand. It is a sad thing that Molly is so strange.

Sometimes, but not very often, a boy or a girl comes home again, like a frightened child to a mother. America is too hard for some of us. These are beaten and return to the old poverty, preferring it because the ways of Irish poverty are less strenuous than the ways of American success. Sometimes, but this is rare too, a young man or woman returns, not beaten, but satisfied with moderate success. These bring with them money; the girl a marriage-portion for herself, the man enough to restock his father's farm, which he looks to inherit in the future. Sometimes older people come back to buy land, build houses, and settle down. But these are always afterwards strangers in Irish life. They never recapture the spirit of it. They have worked in America, thought in America, breathed in America, America has marked them as hers, and they are ours no longer though they come back to us.

Often we have passing visits from those who left us. The new easiness of travelling and the comparative comfort of the journey make these visits commoner than they were. Our friends come back for two months or three. It is wonderful to see how quickly they seem to fall into the old ways. The young man, who was perhaps an insurance agent in New York, will fold away his city clothes and turn to with a loy at cutting turf. The girl, who got out of the train so fine to look at that her own father hardly dared to greet her, will be out next day in the fields making hay with her sisters and brothers.

But there is a restlessness about these visitors of ours. They want us to do new things. They find much amiss which we had not noticed. They are back with us, and glad to be back; but America is calling them all the time. There is very much that we cannot give. Soon they will go again, and any tears shed at the second parting are ours, not theirs.

There are many histories of Ireland, dealing sometimes with the whole, sometimes with this or that part of her story. They are written with the passion of patriots, with the bitterness of enemies, with the blind fury of partisans, with the cold justice of scientific men who stand aloof. None of them are wholly satisfactory as histories of England are, or histories of America. No one can write a history of Ireland which will set forth intelligibly Ireland's place in the world. We wait for the coming of some larger-minded man who will write the history, not of Ireland, but of the Irish. In one respect it is not with us as it is with other nations. Their stories centre in their homes. Their conquerors go forth, but return again. Their thinkers live amid the scenes on which their eyes first opened. Their contributions to human knowledge are connected in all men's minds with their own lands. The statesmen of other nations rule their own people, build empires on which their own flag flies. The workmen of other nations, captains of industry or sweating labourers, make wealth in their home lands. It has never been so with us.

Our historian, when he comes and writes of us, may take as the motto of his book, Virgil's comment on the honey-making of the bees: "Sic vos non vobis." [Thus do ye, but not for yourselves.] Long ago we spread the gospel of the Cross over the dark places of Europe. The monasteries of our monks, the churches of our missionary preachers were everywhere. But our own land is still the prey of that acrimonious theological bitterness which is, of all things, the most utterly opposed to the spirit of Christ. So we, but not for ourselves, made sweetness. Kant is a German. Bergson is a Frenchman. All the world knows it. Who knows or cares that John Scotus Erigena or Bishop Berkeley were Irish? The greatness of their names has shed no lustre over us. Our captains and soldiers have fought and won under every flag in Europe, and under the stars and stripes of America. Under our own flag they rarely fought and never won. Statesmen of our race have been among the governors of almost every nation under the sun. Our own land we have never governed yet. The names of Swift, of Goldsmith, of Sheridan, of a score of other men of letters, add to the glory of the record of English literature, not of ours. Our people, by their toil of mind and muscle, have made other lands rich in manufacture and commerce. Ireland remains poor.

That is why there is not, and cannot be, a history of Ireland. It is never in Ireland that our history has been made. The threads of our story are ours—spun at home—but they are woven into splendid fabrics elsewhere, not in Ireland. But the history of the Irish people will be a great work when it is written. There will be strange chapters in it, and none stranger than those which tell of our part in the making of America. It will be a record of mingled good and evil, but it will always have in it the elements of high romance. From the middle of the eighteenth century, when the tide of emigration set westwards from Ulster, down to to-day, when, with slackening force, it flows from Connaught, those who went have always been the men and women for whom life at home seemed hopeless. There was no promise of good for them here. But in spite of the intolerable sadness of their going, in spite of the fact that at home they were beaten men, there was in them some capacity for doing things. We can succeed, it seems, elsewhere, but not here. This is the strange law which has governed our history. We recognise its force everywhere for centuries back. America gives the latest example of its working. An Irishman returns from a visit to America wondering, despairing, hoping. The wonder is in him because he knows those who went and has seen the manner of their going. Success for them seemed impossible, yet very often they have succeeded. The despair is in him because he knows that it has been always in other lands, not in their own, that our people succeed, and because there is no power which can alter the decrees of destiny. But hope survives in him, flickering, because what our people can do elsewhere they can certainly do at home if only we can discover the solution of the malignant riddle of our failure.

James O'Rourke's First Day in New York

[JOHN MCELGUN]

After a comparatively safe and speedy passage, James O'Rourke reached New York. It was one of those mellow days in the early fall when everything looks so serene and calm that the anxious passengers were landed. How beautiful New York Harbor looked! The waters seemed asleep on the bosom of the bay, save where disturbed by the lively ferry-boats ploughing their way backwards and forwards in every direction, and the little snorting tugs, puffing in and out here and there, busy as bees of a June morning. A number of large, majestic-looking ships, that had just come in from all ports of the world, lay out in the stream, looking weary after their long voyage.

It being early day, the passengers were not delayed at Castle Garden overnight, except such as chose to wait for friends who were expecting them. James had no friends, and he walked into the streets and up along Broadway, wondering at the size, and beauty, and cheerful look of the buildings along that noble thoroughfare. It was at the time of day when Broadway is at its liveliest, lined with wagons, carriages, carts, and drays, and the sidewalk so crowded with people hurrying along that it is impossible for any of them to make much speed. James walked on—he knew not where—looking on himself as the most lonely and friendless of the great throng. At length he came to what seemed to him a neglected waste of ground, which, having mortally offended the city in some way, was left behind, forgotten, haggard, and cheerless. Near the centre of this waste stood a large building in a half-finished state, looking so dreary that the ill fate of the neighborhood seemed to have visited it at last.

A number of men were standing around the doors or sitting on the steps of the building, and all looking so much like men that had nothing to do, that James thought it might not inconvenience any of them much to tell him where he might find work. So approaching a gentleman with a wide-leafed straw hat, a tight-fitting coat, much too short for him, and very long, wide pantaloons, who stood on the end of a row picking his teeth, James asked:

"Please, sir, can you tell me where I may find employment? I am a stranger here."

"Most undoubtedly, sir; follow me," said the gentleman, putting his tooth-pick in his vest pocket. "Come along, sir."

James, delighted beyond measure at this sudden good luck, hurried after his new friend, but found it no very easy task to keep up with him. He had such a happy method of diving past crowds which jostled against the other that he had once or twice to wait for him on the corner. At length the gentleman swept into a low, narrow door in one of the side streets, and when James rushed in after him, he found him seated behind a neat little desk, looking as composed as if he had been sitting there since morning.

"So you want employment, do you?" said he, surveying James from head to foot.

"Yes, sir," replied the latter.

"What kind do you prefer?" said he, opening a book which lay on the desk before him. "We have a variety."

"Well, sir," replied James with a smile, "I am not afraid of any kind of work, but would of course prefer whichever pays best."

"Let me see," said the other, closing his eyes and

resting his chin on his hand, "let me see. You are strong enough to work in a dry-goods store?"

"You mean, sir—"

"I mean what you call a cloth-shop in the Old Country."

"Oh! yes; I beg your pardon, sir," said James, greatly elated. "Certainly I am, sir."

"You landed this morning, eh?" said the gentlemen.

"This morning, sir?"

"Any friends in New York?"

"No, sir."

"All alone, eh?"

"Quite so, sir."

"Well, now, sir, I'll tell you what I'll do. You give me three dollars, and I'll send you right up to the establishment."

James felt greatly surprised at this, for he really thought the gentleman was an extensive employer himself. He had never heard of an "intelligence office," and was quite at a loss what to think. He couldn't be a swindler, having such a handsome place.

"No; he *must* be an employer, and probably, wants this money as security for a day or two, till he sees how I get on," thought James.

And looking at the gentleman again, and seeing him busy writing, and apparently utterly oblivious of his presence, was confirmed in this latter idea.

"I'll pay the money, sir," said he, taking from his pocket a few shillings and one half-crown, which was his entire store.

The gentleman thought it most remarkable, but nevertheless it was true, that the coins when changed into dollars amounted to just the required number and ten cents over. So he swept it into a drawer, and, throwing a ten-cent stamp on the desk, drew a piece of paper to him, and, having written a few words on it with violet ink, handed it to James. The latter glanced at it and said:

"What way am I to go there, sir?"

"You see I am so busy, or I would take you up myself. But, anyway, all you have to do is to cross over five blocks to your right, then down a long street you'll see with a marble building on the up-town corner, then one block to your right, then take the cars—you know the street-cars—and ride eleven blocks more, and any one can point out Van Sleuthers & Duckey's dry-goods store to you. Go inside, and show them that address, and you're all right."

James thanked him, left the office, and went in search of Van Sleuthers & Duckey's.

That he did not find it, and that there was no such firm in the city, it is needless to say. He had been swindled out of the last penny by an "intelligence agent"; and after travelling up and down the streets, looking at every sign, stopping to make enquiries at every clothing establishment, he found himself at nightfall close by the East River, footsore, weary, and dejected. He sat down on a log on one of the docks, and, covering his eyes with his hands, began to think over his forlorn, desolate state.

In a large city, without a friend, without one face he had ever known, without a single penny in his pocket. Where to spend the night or get a morsel to eat he knew not; he had spent the ten cents riding up and down in search of Van Sleuthers & Duckey's. He sat a prey to these thoughts for some time, till, raising his head, he saw coming leisurely towards him, from the direction of the street, a man in his shirt-sleeves, smoking a large briarwood pipe.

As he approached, James could see he was of his own race, and made up his mind to speak to him. This was no difficult matter, for the stranger came on, puffing like an engine, and, sitting down beside him, remarked it was a fine night.

O'Rourke saw at once, from his large, rough hands, that he belonged to the working-class, and, observing his neat white shirt and black tie, and everything he wore so clean, thought of the miserable appearance of the English workingmen.

"You're not long out from the ould counthry, I think," said he kindly.

"No, indeed," said James. "I came ashore this morning."

"Well, well," said the man, moving close to him, "I am glad to see any one so late from the ould dart. How is things there now; anything better?"

"Oh! much the same as usual," replied James. "Improvements come very slowly in Ireland."

"That's so, that's so, me friend," said the other, with a sigh. "But the people an't starving as they wor when I left there?"

"Not so bad as that now," said James.

"Do you live around here?" asked the stranger, after a pause.

"I have no home," said James, drawing back his head a little.

"No home," said the other, "and a greenhorn; why, that's rough. I suppose be that ye mane you haven't got any money neither."

"Not a penny," was the reply.

Then James told him how he had been cheated by the intelligence agent.

"You're not the first who has been fleeced by thim robbers," said the other in a rage. "They swindle dozens of poor innocent people every day, and you'll niver hear of one of thim bein' arristed. But," added he, checking himself, "it can't be helped now, and I'll niver see one of my countrymen that desarves it out in the streets at night while I have a room; so you must come wid me to-night. The ould woman 'ill find some place for you to sleep."

James thanked him again and again, and, after enjoying a smoke from his pipe, they walked up the dock and along the street a little way, till they came to a somewhat neat-looking brick house with a wooden stoop. The man entered, and both went up a flight of very clean but carpetless stairs to the third story, and, turning the knob of the door, entered a tidily furnished room of comfortable dimensions. Over the wooden mantel-piece hung a handsome engraving of Archbishop Hughes, side by side with another of St. Patrick, and on the opposite wall hung a picture of Killarney Lakes. Several other pictures, some of Irish clergy, some of American, were fastened round the walls, all very tastefully arranged.

There was no person in the room on their entrance, and the man, seeing James look closely at the archbishop's likeness, began to tell numerous stories of his kindness and benevolence. After some time, a woman came in, carrying a basket on her arm; and from the appearance of her face, and the trim, cleanly way in which she was clad, James knew at once whose taste had arranged the room.

"Well, well, Terence, and what a man you are," said she, laying down the basket, and looking at her husband with a smile, "to leave housekeeping."

"Oh! In troth, I was afraid she'd begin to screech whin ye'd be gone, Bridget, so I left her inside with Mrs. Kearney. She stays as quiet wid her as wid yourself," said her husband.

"Oh! just so; anything to get rid of the job. But keep quiet now; she's asleep in Mrs. Kearney's arms, and I'll bring her in and put her in the cradle."

The woman left the room, and soon returned, carrying in her arms a little babe of a few months old, and, shaking her hand at her husband to say nothing, lest he should rouse the infant, went through the passage-way into another room.

The man conversed with James for awhile, then, telling him he'd be back in a moment, followed his wife. Both soon returned, and James could see from the kind, sympathetic look the woman gave him that her husband had been telling his story.

"Excuse me," said the man, "but ye haven't tould me yer name."

James told him.

"In troth, and a good name it is. My own is Terence McManus, and this is Mrs. McManus, and that sleepy youngster ye seen a minute ago is Mary McManus. So we know each other all roun' now, and are quite at our aise."

The agreeable, honest, good-natured manner of the man did make James feel much easier in mind than he had felt for some time. Mrs. McManus prepared a good meal, of which all three partook. This over, they sat together, and talked over matters in the old and new country. One important point to James came out from this conversation, and that was he learned that his host, who worked along the docks, being what is commonly called a 'longshoreman, would find him employment at the same business the following day.

Boyne Water and Bad Blood and *The Freedom Picnic*

[FINLEY PETER DUNNE]

"Jawn," said Mr. Dooley to Mr. McKenna, "what did th' Orangeys do to-day?"

"They had a procession," said Mr. McKenna.

"Was it much, I dinnaw?"

"Not much."

"That's good," said Mr. Dooley. "That's good. They don't seem to be gettin' anny sthronger, praise be! Divvle th' sthraw do I care f'r thim. They niver harmed hair nor head iv me; an' they ain't likely to, ayether, so long as th' R-road keeps th' way it is. Faith, 'twud be a fine pot iv porridge th' like iv thim 'd ate if they come up into Ar-rchey Road. I'm an ol' man, Jawn—though not so ol' at that—but I'd give tin years iv me life to see an Orange procession west on Ar-rchey Road with th' right flank restin' on Halsthed Sthreet. It'd rest there. Th' Lord knows it wud.

"Jawn, I have no dislike to th' Orangeys. Nawthin' again thim. I'd not raise me hand to thim, I wud not, though me cousin Tim was kilt be wan iv thim dhroppin' a bolt on his skull in th' ship-yards in Belfast. 'Twas lucky f'r that there Orangey he spoke first. Me cousin Tim had a ship-ax in his hand that 'd 've evened things up f'r at laste wan iv th' poor pikemen that Sarsfield had along with him. But I've nawthin' again thim at that but th' wan that kilt Tim. I'd like to meet that lad in some quite place like th' Clan-na-Gael picnic on th' fifteenth iv August, some place where we'd have fair play.

"Jawn, live an' let live is me motto. On'y I say this here, that 'tis a black disgrace to Chicago f'r to let th' likes iv thim thrapze about th' sthreets with their cheap ol' flags an' ribbons. Oh dear, oh dear, if Pathrick's Day on'y come some year on' th' twelfth day iv July! Where'd they be, where'd they be?

"D'ye know things is goin' to th' dogs in this town, Jawn, avick? Sure they are, faith. I mind th' time well whin an Orangey'd as lave go through hell in a celluloid suit as march in this here town on the twelfth iv July. I raymimber wanst they was a man be th' name iv Morgan Dempsey—a first cousin iv thim Dempseys that lives in Cologne Sthreet—an' he was a Roscommon man, too, an' wan iv th' cutest divvles that iver breathed th' breath iv life.

"Well, whin th' day come f'r th' Orangeys to cilly-
brate th' time whin King Willum—may th' divvle
hould him!—got a stand-off—an' 'twas no betther,
Jawn, f'r th' Irish 'd 've skinned him alive if th' poor
ol' gaby iv an English king hadn't ducked—What's
that? Don't I know it? I have a book at home written
be an impartial historyan, Pathrick Clancy Duffy, to
prove it. What was I sayin'? Whin' th' twelfth day iv
July come around an' th' Orangeys got ready to cilly-
brate th' day King Willum, with all his Gatlin' guns
an' cannon, just barely sthud off Sarsfield an' his men
that had on'y pikes an' brickbats an' billyard cues, th'
good people was infuryated. I dinnaw who was th'
mayor in thim days. He was niver ilicted again. But,
annyhow, he give it out that th' Orangeys' procission
must not be hurted. An' all th' newspapers asked th'
good people to be quite, an' it was announced at high
mass an' low mass that annywan that sthruck a blow
'd be excommunicated.

"Well, ye know how it is whin modheration is
counselled, Jawn. Modheration is another name f'r
murdheration. So they put two platoons iv polismin
in front iv th' Orangeys an' three behind, an' a double column alongside; an' away they wint.

"No wan intherfered with thim; an' that didn't
plaze Morgan Dempsey, who'd served his time a
calker in a ship-yard. Bein' iv a injaneyous disposi-
tion, he made up his mind f'r to do something to

show that pathrietism wasn't dead in this counthry. So he got up in a hallway in Washington Sthreet, an' waited. Th' procission come with th' polismen in front an' behind an' along th' sides, an' th' German Band, thryin' to keep wan eye on the house-tops on both sides iv th' sthreet, an' to read th' music iv 'Lillibullero' an' 'Croppies lie down' an' 'Boyne Wather' with th' other. Th' Orangeys didn't look up. They kept their eyes pointed sthraight ahead, I'll say that f'r thim. They're murdherin' vilyans; but they're Irish, iv a sort.

"Whin they come by Dempsey, he pokes his head out iv th' dure; an' says he, 'Th' 'ell with all th' Prowtestant bishops.' Now that same over in Derry'd have had all th' tilin's in town flyin'; but th' Orangeys 'd been warned not to fight, an' they wint sthraight on, on'y they sung 'Lillibullero.' Did ye niver hear it? It goes (*singing*) 'Ho! Brother Teigue, dost hear in th' degree?'

"Th' Lor f'rgive me f'r singin' it, Jawn. See if there's anny wan near th' dure.

"Well, whin they got through, Dempsey puts his hands to his mouth, an' yells, 'Th' 'ell with King Willum.' That was more thin th' Orangeys cud stand. They halted as wan man, an' roared out, 'Th' 'ell with th' pope.' 'What's that?' says th' captain iv th' polis foorce. He was a man be th' name of Murphy, an' he was blue with rage f'r havin' to lead th' Orangeys. 'Ma-arch on, Brass Money,' says th' Orange marshal. Murphy pulled him fr'm his horse; an' they wint at it, club an' club. Be that time th' whole iv th' line was ingaged. Ivry copper belted an Orangey; an' a sergeant named Donahue wint through a whole lodge, armed on'y, Jawn, with a clarinet an' wan cymbal. He did so. An' Morgan Dempsey, th' cute divvle, he sthood by, an' encouraged both sides. F'r, next to an Orangey, he likes to see a polisman kilt. That ended wan Orangey parade.

"Not that I think it was right. I suppose they ought to be left walk about, an' I'm a fair man. If th' blackest iv thim wint by now, I'd not raise me hand"—

"Hello," says Mr. McKenna, "here goes Killen, the Armagh man. They say he digs with his left foot."

"Jawn," said Mr. Dooley, eagerly, "if ye run up on th' roof, ye'll find th' bricks loose in th' top row iv th' chimbley. Ye might hand him a few."

THE FREEDOM PICNIC

"There's wan thing about th' Irish iv this town," said Mr. Dooley.

"The police?" said Mr. McKenna.

"No," said the philosopher. "But they give picnics that does bate all. Be hivins, if Ireland cud be freed be a picnic, it'd not on'y be free to-day, but an impire, begorra, with Tim Haley, th' Banthry man, evictin' Lord Salisb'ry fr'm his houldin'. 'Twud that.

"Jawn, th' la-ads have got th' thrick iv freein' Ireland down to a sinsible basis. In th' ol' days they wint over with dinnymite bumbs in their pockets, an' ayether got their rowlers on thim in Cork an' blew thimsilves up or was arrested in Queenstown f'r disordherly conduct. 'Twas a divvle iv a risky job to be a pathrite in thim days, an' none but those that had no wan dipindint on thim cud afford it. But what was th' use? Ireland wint on bein' th' same opprissed green oil it had always been, an' th' on'y difference th' revolutions made was ye sa-aw new faces on th' bridges an' th' Wolfe Tones passed another set iv resolutions.

"'Tis different now. Whin we wants to smash th' Sassenach an' restore th' land iv th' birth iv some iv us to her thrue place among th' nations, we gives a picnic. 'Tis a dam sight asier thin goin' over with a slug iv joynt powder an' blowin' up a polis station with no wan in it. It costs less; an', whin 'tis done, a man can lep aboord a sthreet ca-ar, an' come t his family an' sleep it off.

"I wint out last Choosdah, an' I suppose I must've freed as much as eight counties in Ireland. All th' la-ads was there. Th' first ma-an I see was Dorgan, the sanyor guarjeen in the Wolfe Tone Lithry

Society. He's th' la-ad that have made th' Prince iv
Wales thrimble in his moccasins. I heerd him wanst
makin' a speech that near injooced me to take a
bumb in me hand an' blow up Westminsther
Cathedral. 'A-re ye,' he says, 'men, or a-re ye slaves?'
he says. 'Will ye,' he says, 'set idly by,' he says, 'while
th' Sassenach,' he says, 'has th' counthry iv Immitt
an' O'Connell,' he says, 'an' Jawn Im Smyth,' he
says, 'undher his heel?' he says. 'Arouse,' he says,
'slaves and despots!' he says. 'Clear th' way!' he says.
'Cowards an' thraitors!' he says. 'Faugh-a-ballagh!'
he says. He had th' beer privilege at th' picnic, Jawn.

"Hinnissy, th' plumber, who blew wan iv his fingers
off with a bumb intinded f'r some iv th' archytecture
iv Liverpool, had th' conthract f'r runnin' th'
knock-th'-babby-down-an'-get-a-nice-seegar jint.
F'r the good iv th' cause I knocked th' babby down,
Jawn, an' I on'y wishth' Queen iv England 'r th'
Prince iv Wales cud be injooced to smoke wan iv th'
seegars. Ye might as well go again a Roman candle.
Th' wan I got was made iv baled hay, an' 'twas
rumored about th' pa-ark that Hinnissy was wur-
rukin' off his surplus stock iv bumbs on th'
pathrites. His cousin Darcey had th' shootin' gallery
privilege, an' he done a business th' like iv which
was niver knowed be puttin' up th' figure iv an Irish
polisman f'r th' la-ads to shoot at. 'Twas bad in th'
end though, f'r a gang iv Tipp'rary lads come along

behind th' tent an' begun thrown stones at th' copper. Wan stone hit a Limerick man, an' th' cry 'butther-milk' wint around; an' be hivins, if it hadn't been that th' chief iv polis, wise la-ad, sint none but German polismen to th' picnic, there'd not been a man left to tell th' tale."

"What's that all got to do with freeing Ireland?" asked Mr. McKenna.

"Well, 'tis no worse off thin it was befure, anny-how," said Mr. Dooley.

The Green Flag

[ARTHUR CONAN DOYLE]

When Jack Conolly, of the Irish Shotgun Brigade, the Rory of the Hills Inner Circle, and the extreme left wing of the Land League, was incontinently shot by Sergeant Murdoc of the constabulary, in a little moonlight frolic near Kanturk, his twin brother Dennis joined the British Army. The countryside had become too hot for him; and, as the seventy-five shillings were wanting which might have carried him to America, he took the only way handy of getting himself out of the way. Seldom has Her Majesty had a less promising recruit, for his hot Celtic blood seethed with hatred against Britain and all things British. The Sergeant, however, smiling complacently over his six feet of brawn and his forty-four-inch chest, whisked him off with a dozen other of the boys to the depôt at Fermoy, whence in a few weeks they were sent on, with the spade-work kinks taken out of their backs, to the first battalion of the Royal Mallows, at the top of the roster for foreign service.

The Royal Mallows, at about that date, were as strange a lot of men as ever were paid by a great empire to fight its battles. It was the darkest hour of the land struggle, when the one side came out with crowbar and battering-ram by day, and the other with mask and with shot-gun by night. Men driven from their homes and potato-patches found their way even into the service of the Government, to which it seemed to them that they owed their troubles, and now and then they did wild things before they came. There were recruits in the Irish regiments who would forget to answer to their own names, so short had been their acquaintance with them. Of these the Royal Mallows had their full share; and, while they still retained their fame as being one of the smartest corps in the Army, no one knew better than their officers that they were dry-rotted with treason and with bitter hatred of the flag under which they served.

And the centre of all the disaffection was C Company, in which Dennis Conolly found himself enrolled. They were Celts, Catholics, and men of the tenant class to a man; and their whole experience of the British Government had been an inexorable landlord, and a constabulary who seemed to them to be always on the side of the rent-collector. Dennis was not the only moonlighter in the ranks, nor was he alone in having an intolerable family blood-feud to harden his heart. Savagery had begotten savagery in that veiled civil war. A landlord with an iron mortgage weighing down upon him had small bowels for his tenantry. He did but take what the law allowed; and yet, with men like Jim Holan, or Patrick McQuire, or Peter Flynn, who had seen the roofs torn from their cottages and their folk huddled among their pitiable furniture upon the roadside, it was ill to argue about abstract law. What matter that in that long and bitter struggle there was many another outrage on the part of the tenant, and many another grievance on the side of the landowner! A stricken man can only feel his own wound, and the rank and file of the C Company of the Royal Mallows were sore and savage to the soul. There were low whisperings in barrack-rooms and canteens, stealthy meetings in public-house parlours, bandying of passwords from mouth to mouth, and many other signs which made their officers right glad when the order came which sent them to foreign, and better still to active, service.

For Irish regiments have before now been disaffected, and have at a distance looked upon the foe as though he might, in truth, be the friend; but when they have been put face on to him, and when their officers have dashed to the front with a wave and a halloo, those rebel hearts have softened and their gallant Celtic blood has boiled with the mad joy of fight, until the slower Britons have marvelled that they ever could have doubted the loyalty of their Irish comrades. So it would be again, according to the officers, and so it would not be if Dennis Conolly and a few others could have their way.

～

It was a March morning upon the eastern fringe of the Nubian desert. The sun had not yet risen; but a tinge of pink flushed up as far as the cloudless zenith, and the long strip of sea lay like a rosy ribbon across the horizon. From the coast inland stretched dreary sand-plains, dotted over with thick clumps of mimosa scrub and mottled patches of thorny bush. No tree broke the monotony of that vast desert. The dull, dusty hue of the thickets and the yellow glare of the sand were the only colours, save at one point where, from a distance, it seemed that a landslip of snow-white stones had shot itself across a low foot-hill. But as the traveller approached he saw, with a thrill, that these were no stones, but the bleaching bones of a slaughtered army. With its dull tints, its gnarled viprous bushes, its arid, barren soil, and this death-streak trailed across it, it was indeed a nightmare country.

Some eight or ten miles inland the rolling plain curved upwards with a steeper slope until it ran into a line of red basaltic rock which zig-zagged from north to south, heaping itself up at one point into a fantastic knoll. On the summit of this there stood upon that March morning three Arab chieftains— the Sheik Kadra of the Hadendowas, Moussa Wad Aburhegel, who led the Berber dervishes, and Hamid Wad Hussein, who had come northward with his fighting men from the land of the Baggaras. They had all three just risen from their praying-carpets, and were peering out, with fierce, high-nosed faces thrust forwards, at the stretch of country revealed by the spreading dawn.

The red rim of the sun was pushing itself now above the distant sea, and the whole coastline stood out brilliantly yellow against the rich deep blue beyond. At one spot lay a huddle of white-walled houses, a mere splotch in the distance; while four tiny cock-boats, which lay beyond, marked the position of three of Her Majesty's ten-thousand-ton troopers and the Admiral's flagship. But it was not upon the distant town, nor upon the great vessels, nor yet upon the sinister white litter which gleamed in the plain beneath them, that the Arab chieftains gazed. Two miles from where they stood, amid the sand-hills and the mimosa scrub, a great parallelo-gram had been marked by piled-up bushes. From the inside of this dozens of tiny blue smoke-reeks curled up into the still morning air; while there rose from it a confused deep murmur, the voices of men and the gruntings of camels blended into the same insect buzz.

"The unbelievers have cooked their morning food," said the Baggara chief, shading his eyes with his tawny, sinewy hand. "Truly their sleep has been but scanty; for Hamid and a hundred of his men have fired upon them since the rising of the moon."

"So it was with these others," answered the Sheik Kadra, pointing with his sheathed sword towards the old battle-field. "They also had a day of little water and a night of little rest, and the heart was gone out of them ere ever the sons of the Prophet had looked them in the eyes. This blade drank deep that day, and will again before the sun has travelled from the sea to the hill."

"And yet these are other men," remarked the Berber dervish. "Well, I know that Allah has placed them in the clutch of our fingers, yet it may be that they with the big hats will stand firmer than the cursed men of Egypt."

"Pray Allah that it may be so," cried the fierce Baggara, with a flash of his black eyes. "It was not to chase women that I brought seven hundred men from the river to the coast. See, my brother, already they are forming their array."

A fanfare of bugle-calls burst from the distant camp. At the same time the bank of bushes at one side had been thrown or trampled down, and the little army within began to move slowly out on to the plain. Once clear of the camp they halted, and the slant rays of the sun struck flashes from bayonet and from gun-barrel as the ranks closed up until the big pith helmets joined into a single long white ribbon. Two streaks of scarlet glowed on either side of the square, but elsewhere the fringe of fighting-men was of the dull yellow khaki tint which hardly shows against the desert sand. Inside their array was a dense mass of camels and mules bearing stores and ambulance needs. Outside a twinkling clump of cavalry was drawn up on each flank, and in front a thin scattered line of mounted infantry was already slowly advancing over the bush-strewn plain, halting on every eminence, and peering warily round as men might who have to pick their steps among the bones of those who have preceeded them.

The three chieftains still lingered upon the knoll, looking down with hungry eyes and compressed lips at the dark steel-tipped patch.

"They are slower to start than the men of Egypt," the Sheik of the Hadendowas growled in his beard.

"Slower also to go back, perchance, my brother," murmured the dervish. "And yet they are not many—three thousand at the most."

"And we ten thousand, with the Prophet's grip upon our spear-hafts and his words upon our banner. See to their chieftain, how he rides upon the right and looks up at us with the glass that sees from afar! It may be that he sees this also." The Arab shook his sword at the small clump of horsemen who had spurred out from the square.

"Lo! he beckons," cried the dervish; "and see those others at the corner, how they bend and heave. Ha! by the Prophet, I had thought it."

As he spoke a little woolly puff of smoke spurted up at the corner of the square, and a seven-pound shell burst with a hard metallic smack just over their heads. The splinters knocked chips from the red rocks around them.

"Bismillah!" cried the Hadendowa; "if the gun can carry thus far, then ours can answer to it. Ride to the left, Moussa, and tell Ben Ali to cut the skin from the Egyptians if they cannot hit yonder mark. And you, Hamid, to the right, and see that three thousand men lie close in the wady that we have chosen. Let the others beat the drum and show the banner of the Prophet; for by the black stone their spears will have drunk deep ere they look upon the stars again."

A long, straggling, boulder-strewn plateau lay on the summit of the red hills, sloping very precipitously to the plain, save at one point, where a winding gully carved downwards, its mouth choked with sand-mounds and olive-hued scrub. Along the edge of this position lay the Arab host, a motley crew of shockheaded desert clansmen, fierce predatory slave-dealers of the interior, and wild dervishes from the Upper Nile, all blent together by their common fearlessness and fanaticism. Two races were there, as wide as the poles apart, the thin-lipped, straight-haired Arab, and the thick-lipped, curly negro; yet the faith of Islam had bound them closer than a blood tie. Squatting among the rocks, or lying thick-ly in the shadow, they peered out at the slow-moving square beneath them, while women with water-skins and bags of dhoora fluttered from group to group, calling out to each other those fighting texts from the Koran which in the hour of battle are madden-ing as wine to the true believer. A score of banners waved over the ragged, valiant crew, and among them, upon desert horses and white Bishareen camels, were the Emirs and Sheiks who were to lead them against the infidels.

As the Sheik Kadra sprang into his saddle and drew his sword there was a wild whoop and a clatter of waving spears, while the one-ended war-drums burst into a dull crash like a wave upon shingle. For a moment ten thousand men were up on the rocks with brandished arms and leaping figures; the next they were under cover, again waiting sternly and silently for their chieftain's orders. The square was less than half a mile from the ridge now, and shell after shell from the seven-pound guns were pitching over it. A deep roar on the right, and then a second one showed that the Egyptian Krupps were in action. Sheik Kadra's hawk eyes saw that the shells burst far beyond the mark, and he spurred his horse along to where a knot of mounted chiefs were gathered round two guns, which were served by their captured crews.

"How is this, Ben Ali?" he cried. "It was not thus that the dogs fired when it was their own brothers in faith at whom they aimed!"

A chieftain reigned his horse back, and thrust a blood-smeared sword into its sheath. Beside him two Egyptian artillerymen with their throats cut were sobbing out their lives upon the ground.

"Who lays the gun this time?" asked the fierce chief, glaring at the frightened gunners. "Here, thou black-browed child of Shaitan, aim, and aim for thy life."

It may have been chance, or it may have been skill, but the third and fourth shells burst over the square. Sheik Kadra smiled grimly and galloped back to the left, where his spearmen were streaming down into the gully. As he joined them a deep growling rose from the plain beneath, like the snarling of a sullen wild beast, and a little knot of tribesmen fell in a struggling heap, caught in the blast of lead from a Gardner. Their comrades pressed on over them, and sprang down into the ravine. From all along the crest burst the hard sharp crackle of Remington fire.

The square had slowly advanced, rippling over the low sandhills, and halting every few minutes to rearrange its formation. Now, having made sure that there was no force of the enemy in the scrub, it changed its direction, and began to take a line parallel to the Arab position. It was too steep to assail from the front, and if they moved far enough to the right the General hoped that he might turn it. On the top of those ruddy hills lay a baronetcy for him, and a few extra hundreds in his pension, and he meant having them both that day. The Remington fire was annoying, and so were those two Krupp guns: already there were more cacolets full than he cared to see. But on the whole he thought it better to hold his fire until he had more to aim at than a few hundred of fuzzy heads peeping over a razor-back ridge. He was a bulky, red-faced man, a fine whist-player, and a soldier who knew his work. His men believed in him, and he had good reason to believe in them, for he had excellent stuff under him that day. Being an ardent champion of the short-service system, he took particular care to work with veteran first battalions, and his little force was the compressed essence of an army corps.

The left front of the square was formed by four companies of the Royal Wessex, and the right by four of the Royal Mallows. On either side the other halves of the same regiments marched in quarter column of companies. Behind them, on the right was a battalion of Guards, and on the left one of Marines, while the rear was closed in by a Rifle battalion. Two Royal Artillery seven-pound screw-guns kept pace with the square, and a dozen white-bloused sailors, under their blue-coated, tight-waisted officers, trailed their Gardner in front, turning every now and then to spit up at the draggled banners which waved over the cragged ridge. Hussars and Lancers scouted in the scrub at each side, and within moved the clump of camels, with humorous eyes and supercilious lips, their comic faces a contrast to the blood-stained men who already lay huddled in the cacolets on either side.

The square was now moving slowly on a line parallel with the rocks, stopping every few minutes to pick up wounded, and to allow the screw-guns and Gardner to make themselves felt. The men looked serious, for that spring on to the rocks of the Arab army had given them a vague glimpse of the number and ferocity of their foes; but their faces were set like stone, for they knew to a man that they must win or they must die—and die, too, in a particularly unlovely fashion. But most serious of all was the General, for he had seen that which brought a flush to his cheeks and a frown to his brow.

"I say, Stephen," said he to his galloper, "those Mallows seems a trifle jumpy. The right flank company bulged a bit when the niggers [*sic*] showed on the hill."

"Youngest troops in the square, sir," murmured the aide, looking at them critically through his eyeglass.

"Tell Colonel Flanagan to see to it, Stephen," said the General; and the galloper sped upon his way. The Colonel, a fine old Celtic warrior, was over at C Company in an instant.

"How are the men, Captain Foley?"

"Never better, sir," answered the senior captain in the spirit that makes a Madras officer look murder if you suggest recruiting his regiment from the Punjab.

"Stiffen them up!" cried the Colonel. As he rode away a colour-sergeant seemed to trip, and fell forward into a mimosa bush.

He made no effort to rise, but lay in a heap among the thorns.

"Sergeant O'Rooke's gone, sorr," cried a voice.

"Never mind, lads," said Captain Foley. "He's died like a soldier, fighting for his Queen."

"To hell with the Queen!" shouted a hoarse voice from the ranks.

But the roar of the Gardner and the typewriter-like clicking of the hopper burst in at the tail of the words. Captain Foley heard them, and Subalterns Grice and Murphy heard them; but there are times when a deaf ear is a gift from the gods.

"Steady, Mallows!" cried the Captain, in a pause of the grunting machine-gun. "We have the honour of Ireland to guard this day."

"And well we know how to guard it, Captain!" cried the same ominous voice; and there was a buzz from the length of the company.

The Captain and the two subs came together behind the marching line.

"They seem a bit out of hand," murmured the Captain.

"Bedad," said the Galway boy, "they mean to scoot like redshanks."

"They nearly broke when the blacks showed on the hill," said Grice.

"The first man that turns, my sword is through him," cried Foley, loud enough to be heard by five files on either side of him. Then, in a lower voice, "It's a bitter drop to swallow, but it's my duty to report what you think to the Chief and have a company of Jollies put behind us." He turned away with the safety of the square upon his mind, and before he had reached his goal the square had ceased to exist.

In their march in front of what looked like a face of cliff, they had come opposite to the mouth of the gully, in which, screened by scrub and boulders, three thousand chosen dervishes, under Hamid Wad Hussein of the Bagarras, were crouching. Tat, tat, tat, went the rifles of three mounted infantrymen in front of the left shoulder of the square, and an instant later they were spurring it for their lives, crouching over the manes of their horses, and pelting over the sandhills with thirty or forty galloping chieftains at their heels. Rocks and scrub and mimosa swarmed suddenly into life. Rushing black figures came and went in the gaps of the bushes. A howl that drowned the shouts of the officers, a long quavering yell, burst from the ambuscade. Two rolling volleys from the Royal Wessex, one crash from the screw-gun firing shrapnel, and then before a second cartridge could be rammed in, a living, glistening black wave tipped with steel, had rolled over the gun, the Royal Wessex had been dashed back among the camels, and a thousand fanatics were hewing and hacking in the heart of what had been the square.

The camels and mules in the centre, jammed more and more together as their leaders flinched from the rush of the tribesmen, shut out the view of the other three faces, who could only tell that the Arabs had got in by the yells upon Allah, which rose ever nearer and nearer amid the clouds of sand-dust, the struggling animals, and the dense mass of swaying, cursing men. Some of the Wessex fired back at the Arabs who had passed them, as excited Tommies will, and it is whispered among doctors that it was not always a Remington bullet which was cut from a wound that day. Some rallied in little knots, stabbing furiously with their bayonets at the rushing spearmen. Others turned at bay with their backs against the camels, and others round the General and his staff, who, revolver in hand, had flung themselves into the heart of it. But the whole square was sidling slowly away from the gorge, pushed back by the pressure at the shattered corner.

The officers and men at the other faces were glancing nervously to their rear, uncertain what was going on, and unable to take help to their comrades without breaking the formation.

"By Jove, they've got through the Wessex!" cried Grice of the Mallows.

"The divils have hurrooshed us, Ted," said his brother subaltern, cocking his revolver.

The ranks were breaking and crowding towards Private Conolly, all talking together as the officers peered back through the veil of dust. The sailors had run their Gardner out, and she was squirting death out of her five barrels into the flank of the rushing stream of savages.

"Oh, this bloody gun!" shouted a voice. "She's jammed again." The fierce metallic grunting had ceased, and her crew were straining and hauling at the breech.

"This damned vertical feed!" cried an officer. "The spanner, Wilson, the spanner! Stand to your cutlasses, boys, or they're into us."

His voice rose into a shriek as he ended, for a shovel-headed spear had been buried in his chest. A second wave of dervishes lapped over the hillocks, and burst upon the machine-gun and the right front of the line. The sailors were overborne in an instant, but the Mallows, with their fighting blood aflame, met the yell of the Moslem with an even wilder, fiercer cry, and dropped two hundred of them with a single point-blank volley. The howling, leaping crew swerved away to the right, and dashed on into the gap which had already been made for them.

But C Company had drawn no trigger to stop that fiery rush. The men leaned moodily upon their Martinis. Some had even thrown them upon the ground. Conolly was talking fiercely to those about him. Captain Foley, thrusting his way through the press, rushed up to him with a revolver in his hand.

"This is your doing, you villain!" he cried.

"If you raise your pistol, Captin, your brains will be over your coat," said a low voice at his side.

He saw that several rifles were turned on him. The two subs. had pressed forward, and were by his side.

"What is it, then?" he cried, looking round from one fierce mutinous face to another. "Are you Irishmen? Are you soldiers? What are you here for but to fight for your country?"

"England is no country of ours," cried several.

"You are not fighting for England. You are fighting for Ireland, and for the Empire of which it is part."

"A black curse on the Impire!" shouted Private McQuire, throwing down his rifle. "'Twas the Impire that backed the man that druv me onto the roadside. May me hand stiffen before I draw thrigger for it."

"What's the Impire to us, Captain Foley, and what's the Widdy to us ayther?" cried a voice.

"Let the constabulary foight for her."

"Ay, be God, they'd be better imployed than pullin' a poor man's thatch about his ears."

"Or shootin' his brother, as they did mine."

"It was the Impire laid my groanin' mother by the wayside. Her son will rot before he upholds it, and ye can put that in the charge-sheet in the next coort-martial."

In vain the three officers begged, menaced, persuaded. The square was still moving, ever moving, with the same bloody fight raging in its entrails. Even while they had been speaking they had been shuffling backwards, and the useless Gardner, with her slaughtered crew, was already a good hundred yards away from them. And the pace was accelerating. The mass of men, tormented and writhing, was trying, by a common instinct, to reach some clearer ground where they could re-form. Three faces were still intact, but the fourth had been caved in, and badly mauled, without its comrades being able to help it. The Guards had met a fresh rush of the Hadendowas, and had blown back the tribesmen with a volley, and the Cavalry had ridden over another stream of them, as they welled out of the gully. A litter of hamstrung horses, and haggled men behind them, showed that a spearman on his face among the bushes can show some sport to the man who charges him. But, in spite of all, the square was still reeling swiftly backwards trying to shake itself clear of this torment which clung to its heart. Would it break, or would it re-form? The lives of five regiments and the honour of the flag hung upon the answer.

Some, at least, were breaking. The C Company of the Mallows had lost all military order and was pushing back in spite of the haggard officers, who cursed and shoved and prayed in the vain attempt to hold them. Their Captain and the subs. were elbowed and jostled, while the men crowded towards Private Conolly for their orders. The confusion had not spread, for the other companies, in the dust and smoke and turmoil, had lost touch with their mutinous comrades. Captain Foley saw that even now there might be time to avert a disaster.

"Think what you are doing, man," he yelled, rushing towards the ringleader. "There are a thousand Irish in the square, and they are dead men if we break."

The words alone might have had little effect on the old moonlighter. It is possible that, in his scheming brain, he had already planned how he was to club his Irish together and lead them to the sea. But at that moment the Arabs broke through the screen of camels which had fended them off. There was a struggle, a screaming, a mule rolled over, a wounded man sprang up in a cacolet with a spear through him, and then through the narrow gap surged a stream of naked savages, mad with battle, drunk with slaughter, spotted and splashed with blood—blood dripping from their spears, their arms, their faces. Their yells, their bounds, their crouching, darting figures, the horrid energy of their spear-thrusts, made them look like a blast of fiends from the pit. And were these the Allies of Ireland? Were these the men who were to strike for her against her enemies? Conolly's soul rose up in loathing at the thought.

He was a man of firm purpose, and yet at the first sight of those howling fiends that purpose faltered, and at the second it was blown to the winds. He saw a huge coal-black negro seize a shrieking camel-driver and saw at his throat with a knife. He saw a shock-headed tribesman plunge his great spear through the back of their own little bugler from Millstreet. He saw a dozen deeds of blood—the murder of the wounded, the hacking of the unarmed—and caught, too, in a glance, the good wholesome faces of the faced-about rear ranks of the Marines. The Mallows, too, had faced about, and in an instant Conolly had thrown himself into the heart of C Company, striving with the officers to form the men up with their comrades.

But the mischief had gone too far. The rank and file had no heart in their work. They had broken before, and this last rush of murderous savages was a hard thing for broken men to stand against. They flinched from the furious faces and dripping fore-arms. Why should they throw away their lives for a flag for which they cared nothing? Why should their leader urge them to break, and now shriek to them to re-form? They would not re-form. They wanted to get to the sea and to safety. He flung himself among them with outstretched arms, with words of reason, with shouts, with gaspings. It was useless; the tide was beyond his control. They were shredding out into the desert with their faces set for the coast.

"Bhoys, will ye stand for this?" screamed a voice. It was so ringing, so strenuous, that the breaking Mallows glanced backwards. They were held by what they saw. Private Conolly had planted his rifle-stock downwards in a mimosa bush. From the fixed bayonet there fluttered a little green flag with the crownless harp. God knows for what black mutiny, for what signal of revolt, that flag had been treasured up within the Corporal's tunic! Now its green wisp stood amid the rush, while three proud regimental colours were reeling slowly backwards.

"What for the flag?" yelled a private.

"My heart's blood for it! and mine! and mine!" cried a score of voices. "God bless it! The flag, boys—the flag!"

C Company were rallying upon it. The stragglers clutched at each other, and pointed. "Here, McQuire, Flynn, O'Hara," ran the shoutings. "Close on the flag! Back to the flag!" The three standards reeled backwards, and the seething square strove for a clearer space where they could form their shattered ranks; but C Company, grim and powder-stained, choked with enemies and falling fast, still closed in on the little rebel ensign that flapped from the mimosa bush.

It was a good half-hour before the square, having disentangled itself from its difficulties and dressed its ranks, began to slowly move forwards over the ground, across which in its labor and anguish it had been driven. The long trail of Wessex men and Arabs showed but too clearly the path they had come.

"How many got into us, Stephen?" asked the General, tapping his snuff-box.

"I should put them down at a thousand or twelve hundred, sir."

"I did not see any get out again. What the devil were the Wessex thinking about? The Guards stood well, though; so did the Mallows."

"Colonel Flanagan reports that his front flank company was cut off, sir."

"Why, that's the Company that was out of hand when we advanced!"

"Colonel Flanagan reports, sir, that the Company took the whole brunt of the attack, and gave the square time to re-form."

"Tell the Hussars to ride forward, Stephen," said the General, "and try if they can see anything of them. There's no firing, and I fear that the Mallows will want to do some recruiting. Let the square take ground by the right, and then advance!"

But the Sheik Kadra of the Hadendowas saw from his knoll that the men with the big hats had rallied, and that they were coming back in the quiet business fashion of men whose work was before them. He took counsel with Moussa the Dervish and

Hussein the Bagarra, and a woestruck man was he when he learned that the third of his men were safe in the Moslem Paradise. So, having still some signs of victory to show, he gave the word, and the desert warriors flitted off unseen and unheard, even as they had come.

A red rock plateau, a few hundred spears and Remingtons, and a plain which for the second time was strewn with slaughtered men, was all that his day's fighting gave to the English General.

It was a squadron of Hussars which came first to the spot where the rebel flag had waved. A dense litter of Arab dead marked the place. Within the flag waved no longer, but the rifle still stood in the mimosa bush, and round it, with their wounds in front, lay the Fenian private and the silent ranks of his Irishry. Sentiment is not an English failing, but the Hussar Captain raised his hilt in a salute as he rode past the blood-soaked ring.

The British General sent home dispatches to his Government, and so did the Chief of the Hadendowas to his, though the stule and manner differed somewhat in each. "The Sheik Kadra of the Hadendowa people to Mohammed Ahmed, the chosen of Allah, homage and greeting," began the latter.

"Know by this that on the fourth day of this moon we gave battle to the Kaffirs who call themselves Inglees, having with us the Chief Hussein with ten thousand of the faithful. By the blessing of Allah we have broken them, and chased them for a mile, though indeed these infidels are different from the dogs of Egypt, and have slain very many of our men. Yet we hope to smite them again ere the new moon be come, to which end I trust that thou wilt send us a thousand Dervishes from Omdurman. In token of our victory I send you by this messenger a flag which we have taken. By the colour it might well seem to have belonged to those of the true faith, but the Kaffirs gave their blood freely to save it, and so we think that, though small, it is very dear to them."

O'Reilly's Great Escape

[ALEXANDER YOUNG]

O'Reilly had made preparations for his escape several months before attempting it. He had told no one of his intention, because he had witnessed so many failures that he decided the safest way was to trust to himself alone. A chance occurrence led him to change his mind. One day while in camp with a convict road party, he had a call from the Rev. Patrick McCabe, a Catholic priest, whose "parish" extended over hundreds of miles of wild Bush country, and whose only parishioners were convicts and ticket-of-leave men. This scholarly, accomplished gentleman had at that time passed fifteen years in ministering to the spiritual needs of convicts, upon whom he exerted a very beneficial influence. His days were almost wholly spent in the saddle, riding alone from camp to camp, and the nights found him wrapped in his blanket under the trees. He was kind to all men, whatever their creed, and a sincere Christian worker. O'Reilly, who had found him a warm friend during his stay in the penal colony, thus bears witness to his usefulness: "He was the best influence; indeed, in my time, he was the only good influence, on the convicts in the whole district of Bunbury." O'Reilly told him his plans of escape as they walked together in the Bush. "It is an excellent way to commit suicide," said the thoughtful priest, who refused to talk about or countenance it. He mounted his horse to say good-by, and, leaning from the saddle toward O'Reilly, he said: "Don't think of that again. Let me think out a plan for you. You'll hear from me before long." Weeks and months passed, and O'Reilly never heard from him. It was a weary waiting, but the convict, though tortured by the uncertainty which kept him from working his own plan, and even hindered him from sleep, still had confidence in his absent and silent friend and adviser.

O'Reilly was exempt from the hardships of labor with the criminal gang on the roads, but had charge of their stores and carried the warden's weekly report to the Bunbury depot. While trudging along with this report one day he reached a plain called the "Race Course." As he was crossing it he heard a "coo-ee," or bush-cry. Looking wistfully in the direction of the sound, he saw a stalwart man coming toward him with an axe on his shoulder. There was a pleasant smile on his handsome face as he approached O'Reilly and said: "My name is Maguire; I'm a friend of Father Mac's, and he's been speaking about you." Having learned the importance of distrusting strangers in convict land, O'Reilly said but a few words and those such as could not reveal his relations with the priest. Observing his hesitation, the stranger took a card from his wallet on which was a message addressed to O'Reilly in the handwriting of Father McCabe. This set at rest all doubts and fears of the man's intentions. O'Reilly eagerly listened to what he had to say, for he had come to carry out the good priest's plan of escape. He said he was clearing the race course, and would be at work there for a month. In February—it was then December—American whalers would touch at Bunbury for water, and he should arrange with one of them to secrete O'Reilly on board and take him out of danger. This was cheering news, but, during the week which passed before he again saw Maguire, O'Reilly could hardly sleep for fear that the man would shrink, when the time came, from the danger to his own life of helping him to escape. But Maguire's hearty and confident manner when he next saw him helped to dispel these fears. "You'll be a free man in February," he said, "as sure as my name is Maguire."

December and January passed away, and a wood-cutter chancing to go to the convict-road camp mentioned the fact that three American whaling barks had put into Bunbury. The news made O'Reilly terribly anxious lest the plan for his escape should fall through. He determined to venture out by himself if he heard nothing from his friends. On returning from the depot, to which he had carried his weekly report, as usual, O'Reilly found Maguire waiting for him at the race course. "Are you ready?" were the faithful fellow's first words. He then said that one of the whalers, the bark *Vigilant,* of New Bedford, was to sail in four days and that Captain Baker had agreed to take O'Reilly on board if he fell in with him outside Australian waters, and had even promised to cruise for two or three days and keep a lookout for him. Maguire had arranged all the details of the escape. O'Reilly was to leave his hut at eight o'clock in the evening of February 18, and take a cut through the Bush on a line which was likely to mislead the native trackers. He had obtained a pair of freeman's shoes, as the mark left by the convict's boot could be easily traced. After leaving the camp he was to push on through the Bush in a straight course toward a convict station on the Vasse road. There he was to lie till he heard some one on the road whistle the first bars of "Patrick's Day." The plan was gone over carefully between

Maguire and O'Reilly, every point being repeated till there could be no doubt of their mutual agreement. The two men then separated.

On the evening of February 18 O'Reilly wrote a letter to his father about his intended escape that night, and his purpose, if successful, to go to the United States. Two months afterwards this letter found its way into the Dublin newspapers. At seven o'clock that evening the warden of the convict party went his rounds and looked in upon all the criminals. He saw O'Reilly sitting in his hut as he passed on his return. Soon after a convict came to the hut to borrow some tobacco and remained so long that the host became very nervous. Fortunately the convict went away before eight. As soon as he had gone O'Reilly changed his boots, put out the light, and started on his desperate venture through the Bush.

Though the woods were dark the stars shone brightly overhead. Before he had gone two hundred yards he was startled by discovering that a man was following him. It was a moment of terrible strain for O'Reilly, but with admirable nerve he coolly waited for the fellow to come up. He proved to be a mahogany sawyer named Kelly, whose saw-pit was close to the fugitive's hut. He was a criminal who had been transported for life. "Are you off?" he whispered hoarsely. "I knew you meant it. I saw you talking to Maguire a month ago, and I knew it all."

These words filled O'Reilly with astonishment and alarm, so that he could not speak. He felt that he was in the man's power. He might have already put the police on his track, or he could do so the next day. But the criminal showed a manly sympathy with the youth who had risked so much for freedom. Holding out his hand to O'Reilly he gave him a strong grip, saying, with a quivering, husky voice: "God speed you. I'll put them on the wrong scent tomorrow." The fugitive could not speak the gratitude he felt, so, silently pressing the manly hand, he pushed on again through the woods.

It was eleven o'clock when he reached the old convict station and lay down beneath a great gum tree at the roadside. From his dusky hiding-place he kept an anxious lookout for friends or foes. In about half an hour two men rode by. They seemed to be farmers, but they may have been a patrol of mounted police. Soon after, the sound of horses coming at a sharp trot was heard by the fugitive. They stopped near his resting place, and he heard "Patrick's Day" whistled in low but clear tones. In an instant O'Reilly ran up to the horsemen, who proved to be Maguire and another friend, M——. They had another horse with them, which O'Reilly mounted, and then, without saying a word, the three started off at a gallop for the woods. They rode on in silence for several hours. At last, Maguire, who led the way, reined in his horse, dismounted, and whistled. He was answered by another whistle. In a few minutes three men came up, two of whom turned out to be cousins of Maguire. The third man took the horses and galloped off, but not till he had given O'Reilly a warm shake of the hand, expressive of his good wishes. The three men then formed in Indian file and, to prevent the discovery of their number, the two behind covered the footprints of the leader. After walking for about an hour they reached a dry swamp near the sea.

O'Reilly remained at this place with M——, while the other men went on. He was told that Bunbury was near by and that they had gone for the boat. After waiting half an hour in anxiety lest the plan of escape had been thwarted at the last moment, a light was seen about half a mile away. This disappeared, only to flash out three more times. It was the signal for O'Reilly and his companion to go forward. They went along the road till they came to a bridge where Maguire was waiting for them. The boat was all ready, but the tide being out they had to wade knee-deep through the mud to reach the water. Maguire, who led the way, was soon aboard with O'Reilly. M—— meanwhile remained on the shore, and, when appealed to by Maguire in a whisper to "come on," answered in a trembling voice: "No, I promised my wife not to go in the boat." This led one of Maguire's cousins, who had come aboard before the others, to answer back in a sneering tone: "All right, go home to your wife." Yet M—— did not deserve this taunt of cowardice. He was brave enough when duty called him, as he afterwards showed.

The four men in the boat were careful to pull quietly till there was no danger of their being overheard. Then they bent vigorously to the oars, as if rowing for life. Little was said, but thoughts of what they had at stake were all the deeper for not finding vent in words. By sunrise the boat had got almost out of sight of land, only the tops of the high sandhills being visible. The course was a straight line of forty miles across Geographe Bay. It had been arranged to lie in wait for the *Vigilant* on the further shore, and row toward her as she passed the northern head of the bay. After pulling strongly till near noon the men began to feel the need of food and drink, which from some reason or other had not been provided for their cruise. O'Reilly, who had eaten nothing for twenty-four hours, suffered dreadfully from thirst. Accordingly the boat was run ashore through the surf and pulled high and dry on the beach. The drenching which the men got in doing this gave them temporary relief from thirst. But this soon became so intense that they wandered for hours through the dried swamps in search of water. Hundreds of paper-bark trees were examined for the wished for drink, but not a drop could be found. O'Reilly became alarmed at the burning pain in his chest, which seemed as if its whole inner surface were covered with a blister. As night was coming on they came to a cattle-track, which led to a shallow and muddy pool. But the water was too foul to drink, so they had to content themselves with cooling their faces in it.

As the whaler would not put to sea till morning or perhaps, the following evening, O'Reilly was in sore need of sustenance to keep up his strength. Fortunately there was a man living in a log house a few miles away whom the Maguires knew and thought well of. He was an Englishman named Johnson, and lived on this lonely expanse of coast with no neighbor nearer than forty miles, as keeper of a large herd of buffalo cows. The three men started for his house, leaving O'Reilly in the Bush for safety, but promising that one should return with food and drink as soon as he could get away unobserved. The poor sufferer whom they left behind watched them winding in and out among the sand-hills till they were lost to view. Then he lay down on the sand in a shady spot and tried to sleep. But the terrible blistering pain in his chest made it impossible for him to remain in a reclining position, and he was obliged to get up and walk about. Hours passed and his friends did not return. O'Reilly's sufferings at this time were the worst he ever experienced. In his desperate straits his knowledge and judgment of woodcraft served him in good stead. Recollecting that the natives lived on freshly killed meat when they could get no water, he sought for a tree with 'possum marks. This he soon found and on climbing it secured a large possum by pulling it out of its hole by the tail and striking its head against the tree. He then learned what his subsequent experience confirmed, that this meat was the very best substitute for water. Maguire returned at nightfall, bringing food and a bottle of water. He remained but a short time, thinking it best to go back to the Englishman's house to avoid exciting suspicion. Soon after his departure, O'Reilly made a bed with boughs and leaves on the sand, using the young branches of the peppermint tree in order to keep away ants, snakes, and centipedes. He soon fell into a sound sleep and did not awake till his friends called him the next morning. Yet all this time he was in danger of being tracked by the police.

The party soon started for the beach, which was reached at about nine o'clock. One of the men was sent with a strong glass, which Maguire had brought, to the top of a high hill to keep a lookout for the *Vigilant*. At about one o'clock he came running down with the welcome news that the vessel was steering north, with all sails spread. As no time was to be lost the boat was quickly run out through the surf. The men pulled cheerily toward the headland, for they were confident of reaching it before the bark passed. They had rowed about a couple of hours when she was seen steering straight toward the boat. The men therefore stopped pulling and waited for her to come up. To their intense disappointment she changed her course slightly when within two miles of the boat, as if to avoid them. The men looked on amazed. Maguire repeatedly said that Captain Baker had pledged his word to take them on board, and he could not believe him mean enough to break it. To settle the question one of the men stood up in the boat and hailed the vessel loudly enough to be heard on board. There was no answer. Again the man hailed her, his companions joining in the shout. No sound came back, and the *Vigilant* seemed to be moving a little further off. At last she brought up abreast of the boat, at about three miles distant. As a last resort, Maguire fixed a white shirt on the top of an oar and the men all shouted again. But the *Vigilant* passed on, leaving the boat to its fate.

As the bark gradually receded in the distance, the bitterness of O'Reilly's disappointment was increased by the sense of danger. What could now be done to save him was the thought of every one in the boat, as she was put about and pulled slowly for the shore. Maguire proposed that the boat should be hauled on to the beach and then O'Reilly should be left in the Bush, as before, while the others went on to Johnson's. It was necessary to trust the Englishman with the secret and let him know the hiding-place of the fugitive, for his friends were obliged to go home and arrange for his escape by one of the other whale-ships. This plan was agreed to by the whole party as the best way out of the difficulty. It was evening when they reached the shore. As his three friends left O'Reilly in the secluded sand valley they shook him by the hand and told him to keep up a good heart. They promised that one of them would come from Bunbury in the course of a week to tell him when the whalers would sail. They also said that they should communicate with old Johnson and ask him to bring food and water to the sand valley, which the old man did.

In his nervous desire to get away as soon as possible from the penal colony, O'Reilly brooded over Captain Baker's promise to cruise for his boat if it was not sighted when the *Vigilant* came out. He thought that the captain might not have seen the boat and might be still cruising along the coast on the lookout for it. This idea made him eager to row out again and take the chance of falling in with the vessel. But the boat in which he had ventured before was too heavy for one person to set afloat or row. He asked Johnson's boy, who came the third night, in place of the old man, if his father had a boat. The lad said there was an old dory at the horse range further up the coast, buried in the sand. When the boy had gone O'Reilly walked along the beach for six or seven miles, and at last found the boat. The heat and dry weather had warped her badly, but O'Reilly pulled her carefully into the water and fastened her by a rope of paper bark to a stake driven into the sand, and went back to his hiding-place for the night.

Next morning he ventured out to sea in this frail craft, which he had made water tight by the use of paper bark. In order to keep his stock of meat from spoiling in the hot sun he let it float in the water, fastened by a rope of paper bark to the stern of the boat. The light craft went rapidly forward under his vigorous rowing, and before night had passed the headland and was on the Indian Ocean.

That night on an unknown sea in a mere shell had a strange, weird interest, heightened by the anxious expectations of the seeker for liberty. O'Reilly ceased rowing the next morning, trusting to the northward current to bring him within view of the whale-ship. He suffered a good deal from the blazing rays of the sun and their scorching reflection from the water. To add to his troubles, the meat towing in the water was becoming putrid, and he found that some of the 'possums and kangaroo rats had been taken by sharks in the night. Toward noon he saw a vessel under sail which he knew must be the *Vigilant* and his hopes ran high, as she drew so near to the boat that he could hear voices on her deck. He saw a man aloft on the lookout; but there was no answer to the cry from the boat, and the vessel again sailed off, leaving O'Reilly to sadly watch her fade away into the night. He afterward heard from Captain Baker that, strangely enough, the boat was not seen from the ship.

Being refreshed by the dew and the cool night air, O'Reilly bent to the work of rowing back to shore. There was nothing to do but to get to his hiding-place and await Maguire's return. He tugged at the oars pretty steadily through the night, and when morning came he was within sight of the sand-hills on the headland of Geographe Bay. He reached land by noon and then walked on wearily to Johnson's, where he arrived the same night. The fatigue and anxiety which he had gone through had thoroughly exhausted him. He cared for nothing but sleep, and this he could have without stint in the secluded sand valley. There he remained for five days, when he was cheered by the arrival of Maguire and M——, who said that they had come to see him through. This time Maguire brought a brief letter from Father McCabe, asking O'Reilly to remember him. He had arranged with Captain Gifford, of the bark *Gazelle,* of New Bedford, one of the whalers that were to sail

next day, to take O'Reilly on board. In order to
insure the fulfillment of this agreement the good
Father had paid the captain ten pounds to carry his
friend as far as Java. Unfortunately there was one
serious danger ahead. This was the presence of a
criminal convict, one of the worst characters in the
penal colony, Martin Bowman, or Beaumont, a
ticket-of-leave man. This fellow had discovered
O'Reilly's plan of escape and had threatened to
reveal the whole affair to the police if Maguire did
not take him on board the whale-ship also. As it was
unsafe to refuse this demand, Bowman was unwill-
ingly included in the party.

Soon after daybreak the next morning the men
went down to the beach. Old Johnson and his boy
were there to see them off. They got afloat without
delay, and rowed vigorously toward the headland,
according to Captain Gifford's directions. By noon
they saw the two whaleships under full headway.
Toward evening they were hailed by one of the vessels, and a voice shouted O'Reilly's name and cried
out: "Come on board!" The men were delighted at
this call. They pulled alongside and O'Reilly was
helped out of the boat by the strong arms of Henry
C. Hathaway, the third mate. He was warmly wel-
comed by Captain Gifford, who gave him accom-
modations in his cabin. Martin Bowman, the
escaped criminal, was quartered in the forecastle

with the crew. As the boat pushed off from the ship, Maguire stood up and cried: "God bless you; don't forget us, and don't mention our names till you know it's all over." M——, also, who had so well proved his courage, shouted a kind farewell, which moved the grateful O'Reilly to tears.

The official narrative is briefer. It is found in the *Police Gazette* of the District of Western Australia in the form of the following advertisement:

ABSCONDERS.

20—John B. O'Reilly, registered No. 9843, imperial convict; arrived in the colony per convict ship *Hougoumont* in 1868; sentenced to twenty years, 9th July, 1866. Description— Healthy appearance; present age 25 years; 5 feet 7½ inches high, black hair, brown eyes, oval visage, dark complexion: an Irishman. Absconded from Convict Road Party, Bunbury, on the 18th of February, 1869.

Village Ghosts

[**WILLIAM BUTLER YEATS**]

In the great cities we see so little of the world, we drift into our minority. In the little towns and villages there are no minorities; people are not numerous enough. You must see the world there, perforce. Every man is himself a class; every hour carries its new challenge. When you pass the inn at the end of the village you leave your favorite whimsy behind you; for you will meet no one who can share it. We listen to eloquent speaking, read books and write them, settle all the affairs of the universe. The dumb village multitudes pass on unchanging; the feel of the spade in the hand is no different for all our talk: good seasons and bad follow each other as of old. The dumb multitudes are no more concerned with us than is the old horse peering through the rusty gate of the village pound. The ancient map-makers wrote across unexplored regions, "Here are lions." Across the villages of fishermen and turners of the earth, so different are these from us, we can write but one line that is certain, "Here are ghosts."

My ghosts inhabit the village of H——, in Leinster. History has in no manner been burdened by this ancient village, with its crooked lanes, its old abbey churchyard full of long grass, its green background of small fir-trees, and its quay, where lie a few tarry fishing-luggers. In the annals of entomology it is well known. For a small bay lies westward a little, where he who watches night after night may see a certain rare moth fluttering along the edge of the tide, just at the end of evening or the beginning of dawn. A hundred years ago it was carried here from Italy by smugglers in a cargo of silks and laces. If the moth-hunter would throw down his net, and go hunting for ghost tales or tales of the faeries and such-like children of Lillith, he would have need for far less patience.

To approach the village at night a timid man requires great strategy. A man was once heard complaining, "By the cross of Jesus! how shall I go? If I pass by the hill of Dunboy old Captain Burney may look out on me. If I go round by the water, and up by the steps, there is the headless one and another on the quays, and a new one under the old churchyard wall. If I go right round the other way, Mrs. Stewart is appearing at Hillside Gate, and the devil himself is in the Hospital Lane."

I never heard which spirit he braved, but feel sure it was not the one in the Hospital Lane. In cholera times a shed had been there set up to receive patients. When the need had gone by, it was pulled down, but ever since the ground where it stood has broken out in ghosts and demons and faeries. There is a farmer at H——, Paddy B—— by name—a man of great strength, and a teetotaler. His wife and sister-in-law, musing on his great strength, often wonder what he would do if he drank. One night when passing through the Hospital Lane, he saw what he supposed at first to be a tame rabbit; after a little he found that it was a white cat. When he came near, the creature slowly began to swell larger and larger, and as it grew he felt his own strength ebbing away, as though it were sucked out of him. He turned and ran.

By the Hospital Lane goes the "Faeries' Path." Every evening they travel from the hill to the sea, from the sea to the hill. At the sea end of their path stands a cottage. One night Mrs. Arbunathy, who lived there, left her door open, as she was expecting her son. Her husband was asleep by the fire; a tall man came in and sat beside him. After he had been sitting there for a while, the woman said "In the name of God, who are you?" He got up and went out, saying, "Never leave the door open at this hour, or evil may come to you." She woke her husband and told him. "One of the good people has been with us," said he.

Probably the man braved Mrs. Stewart at Hillside Gate. When she lived she was the wife of the Protestant clergyman. "Her ghost was never known to harm any one," say the village people; "it is only doing a penance upon the earth." Not far from Hillside Gate, where she haunted, appeared for a short time a much more remarkable spirit. Its haunt was the bogeen, a green lane leading from the western end of the village. I quote its history at length: a typical village tragedy. In a cottage at the village end of the bogeen lived a house-painter, Jim Montgomery, and his wife. They had several children. He was a little dandy, and came of a higher class than his neighbors. His wife was a very big woman. Her husband, who had been expelled from the village choir for drink, gave her a beating one day. Her sister heard of it and came and took down one of the window shutters—Montgomery was neat about everything and had shutters on the outside of every window—and beat him with it, being big and strong like her sister. He threatened to prosecute her; she answered that she would break every bone in his body if he did. She never spoke to her sister again, because she had allowed herself to be beaten by so small a man. Jim Montgomery grew worse and worse; his wife soon began to have not enough to eat. She told no one, for she was very proud. Often, too, she would have no fire on a cold night. If any neighbors came in she would say she had let the fire out because she was just going to bed. The people about often heard her husband beating her, but she never told any one. She got very thin. At last one Saturday there was no food in the house for herself and the children. She could bear it no longer, and went to the priest and asked him for some money. He gave her thirty shillings. Her husband met her, and took the money, and beat her. On the following Monday she got very ill, and sent for a Mrs. Kelly. Mrs. Kelly, as soon as she saw her, said, "My woman, you are dying," and sent for the priest and the doctor. She died in an hour. After her death, as Montgomery neglected the children, the landlord had them taken to the workhouse. A few nights after they had gone, Mrs. Kelly was going home through the bogeen when the ghost of Mrs. Montgomery appeared and followed her. It did not leave her until she reached her own house. She told the priest, Father S——, a noted antiquarian, and could not get him to believe her. A few nights afterwards Mrs. Kelly again met the spirit in the same place. She was in too great terror to go the whole way, but stopped at a neighbor's cottage midway, and asked them to let her in. They answered they were going to bed. She cried out, "In the name of God let me in, or I will break open the door." They opened, and so she escaped from the ghost. Next day she told the priest again. This time he believed, and said it would follow her until she spoke to it.

She met the spirit a third time in the bogeen. She asked what kept it from its rest. The spirit said that its children must be taken from the workhouse, for none of its relations were ever there before, and that three masses were to be said for the repose of its soul. "If my husband does not believe you," she said, "show him that," and touched Mrs. Kelly's wrist with three fingers. The places where they touched swelled up and blackened. She then vanished. For a time Montgomery would not believe that his wife had appeared: "She would not show herself to Mrs. Kelly," he said—"she with respectable people to appear to." He was convinced by the three marks, and the children were taken from the workhouse. The priest said the masses, and the shade must have been at rest, for it has not since appeared. Some time afterwards Jim Montgomery died in the workhouse, having come to great poverty through drink.

I know some who believe they have seen the headless ghost upon the quay, and one who, when he passes the old cemetery wall at night, sees a woman with white borders to her cap creep out and follow him. The apparition only leaves him at his own door. The villagers imagine that she follows him to avenge some wrong. "I will haunt you when I die" is a favorite threat. His wife was once half-scared to death by what she considers a demon in the shape of a dog.

These are a few of the open-air spirits; the more domestic of their tribe gather within-doors, plentiful as swallows under southern eaves.

One night a Mrs. Nolan was watching by her dying child in Fluddy's Lane. Suddenly there was a sound of knocking heard at the door. She did not open, fearing it was some unhuman thing that knocked. The knocking ceased. After a little the front-door and then the back-door were burst open, and closed again. Her husband went to see what was wrong. He found both doors bolted. The child died. The doors were again opened and closed as before. Then Mrs. Nolan remembered that she had forgotten to leave window or door open, as the custom is, for the departure of the soul. These strange openings and closings and knockings were warnings and reminders from the spirits who attend the dying.

The house ghost is usually a harmless and well-meaning creature. It is put up with as long as possible. It brings good luck to those who live with it. I remember two children who slept with their mother and sisters and brothers in one small room. In the room was also a ghost. They sold herrings in the Dublin streets, and did not mind the ghost much, because they knew they would always sell their fish easily while they slept in the "ha'nted" room.

I have some acquaintance among the ghost-seers of western villages. The Connaught tales are very different from those of Leinster. These H—— spirits have a gloomy, matter-of-fact way with them. They come to announce a death, to fulfil some obligation, to revenge a wrong, to pay their bills even—as did a fisherman's daughter the other day—and then hasten to their rest. All things they do decently and in order. It is demons, and not ghosts, that transform themselves into white cats or black dogs. The people who tell the tales are poor, serious-minded fishing people, who find in the doings of the ghosts the fascination of fear. In the western tales is a whimsical grace, a curious extravagance. The people who recount them live in the most wild and beautiful scenery, under a sky ever loaded and fantastic with flying clouds. They are farmers and laborers, who do a little fishing now and then. They do not fear the spirits too much to feel an artistic and humorous pleasure in their doings. The ghosts themselves share in their quaint hilarity. In one western town, on whose deserted wharf the grass grows, these spirits have so much vigor that, when a misbeliever ventured to sleep in a haunted house, I have been told they flung him through the window, and his bed after him. In the surrounding villages the creatures use the most strange disguises. A dead old gentleman robs the cabbages of his own garden in the shape of a large rabbit. A wicked sea-captain stayed for years inside the plaster of a cottage wall, in the shape of a snipe, making the most horrible noises. He was only dislodged when the wall was broken down; then out of the solid plaster the snipe rushed away whistling.

Donald and His Neighbours

[ANONYMOUS]

Hudden and Dudden and Donald O'Neary were near neighbours in the barony of Ballinconlig, and ploughed with three bullocks; but the two former, envying the present prosperity of the latter, determined to kill his bullock to prevent his farm being properly cultivated and laboured—that, going back in the world, he might be induced to sell his lands, which they meant to get possession of. Poor Donald, finding his bullock killed, immediately skinned it, and throwing the skin over his shoulder, with the fleshy side out, set off to the next town with it, to dispose of it to the best advantage. Going along the road a magpie flew on the top of the hide, and began picking it, chattering all the time. This bird had been taught to speak and imitate the human voice, and Donald, thinking he understood some words it was saying, put round his hand and caught hold of it. Having got possession of it, he put it under his great-coat, and so went on to the town. Having sold the hide, he went into an inn to take a dram; and, following the landlady into the cellar, he gave the bird a squeeze, which caused it to chatter some broken accents that surprised her very much. "What is that I hear?" said she to Donald. "I think it is talk, and yet I do not understand." "Indeed," said Donald, "it is a bird I have that tells me everything, and I always carry it with me to know when there is any danger. Faith," says he, "it says you have far better liquor than you are giving me." "That is strange," said she, going to another cask of better quality, and asking him if he would sell the bird. "I will," said Donald, "if I get enough for it." "I will fill your hat with silver if you will leave it with me." Donald was glad to hear the news, and, taking the silver, set off, rejoicing at his good luck. He had not been long home when he met with Hudden and Dudden. "Ha!" said he, "you thought you did me a bad turn, but you could not have done me a better: for look here what I have got for the hide," showing them the hatful of silver. "You never saw such a demand for hides in your life as there is at present." Hudden and Dudden that very night killed their bullocks, and set out the next morning to sell their hides. On coming to the place they went to all the merchants, but could only get a trifle for them. At last they had to take what they could get, and came home in a great rage and vowing revenge on poor Donald. He had a pretty good guess how matters would turn out, and his bed being under the kitchen-window, he was afraid they would rob him, or perhaps kill him when asleep; and on that account, when he was going to bed, he left his old mother in his bed, and lay down in her place, which was in the other side of the house, and they, taking the old woman for Donald, choked her in the bed; but he making some noise, they had to retreat and leave the money behind them, which grieved them very much. However, by daybreak, Donald got his mother on his back, and carried her to town. Stopping at a well, he fixed his mother with her staff as if she was stooping for a drink, and then went into a public-house convenient and called for a dram. "I wish," said he to a woman that stood near him, "you would tell my mother to come in. She is at yon well trying to get a drink, and she is hard of hearing: if she does not observe you, give her a little shake, and tell her that I want her." The woman called her several times, but she seemed to take no notice: at length she went to her and shook her by the arm; but when she let her go again, she tumbled on her head into the well, and, as the woman thought, was drowned. She, in great fear and surprise at the accident, told Donald what had happened. "O mercy," said he, "what is this?" He ran and pulled her out of the well, weeping and lamenting all the time, and acting in such a manner that you would imagine that he had lost his senses. The woman, on the other hand, was far worse than Donald: for his grief was only feigned, but she imagined herself to be the cause of the old woman's death. The inhabitants of the town, hearing what had happened, agreed to make Donald up a good sum of money for his loss, as the accident happened in their place; and Donald brought a greater sum home with him than he got for the magpie. They buried Donald's mother; and as soon as he saw Hudden and Dudden, he showed them the last purse of money he had got. "You thought to kill me last night," said he; "but it was good for me it happened on my mother, for I got all that purse for her to make gunpowder."

That very night Hudden and Dudden killed their mothers, and the next morning set off with them to town. On coming to the town with their burden on their backs, they went up and down crying, "Who will buy old wives for gunpowder?" so that every one laughed at them, and the boys at last clodded them out of the place. They then saw the cheat, and vowing revenge on Donald, buried the old women and set off in pursuit of him. Coming to his house, they found him sitting at his breakfast, and seizing him, put him in a sack, and went to drown him in a river at some distance. As they were going along the highway they raised a hare, which they saw had but three feet, and, throwing off the sack, ran after her, thinking by appearance she would be easily taken. In their absence there came a drover that way, and hearing Donald singing in the sack, wondered greatly what could be the matter. "What is the reason," said he, "that you are singing, and you confined?" "Oh, I am going to heaven," said Donald: "and in a short time I expect to be free from trouble." "Oh, dear," said the drover, "what will I give you if you let me to your place?" "Indeed I do not know," said he: "it would take a good sum." "I have not much money," said the drover; "but I have twenty head of fine cattle, which I will give you to exchange places with me." "Well, well," says Donald, "I don't care if I should: loose the sack and I will come out." In a moment the drover liberated him, and went into the sack himself: and Donald drove home the fine heifers and left them in his pasture.

Hudden and Dudden having caught the hare, returned, and getting the sack on one of their backs, carried Donald, as they thought, to the river, and threw him in, where he immediately sank. They then marched home, intending to take immediate possession of Donald's property; but how great was their surprise, when they found him safe at home before them, with such a fine herd of cattle, whereas they knew he had none before? "Donald," said they, "what is all this! We thought you were drowned, and yet you are here before us?" "Ah!" said he, "if I had but help along with me when you threw me in, it would have been the best job ever I met with; for of all the sight of cattle and gold that ever was seen, is there, and no one to own them; but I was not able to manage more than what you see, and I could show you the spot where you might get hundreds." They both swore they would be his friends, and Donald accordingly led them to a very deep part of the river, and lifting up a stone, "Now," said he, "watch this," throwing it into the stream. "There is the very place, and go in, one of you, first, and if you want help you have nothing to do but call." Hudden jumping in, and sinking to the bottom, rose up again, and making a bubbling noise as those do that are drowning, seemed trying to speak but could not. "What is that he is saying now?" says Dudden. "Faith," says Donald, "he is calling for help—don't you hear him? Stand about," continued he, running back, "till I leap in. I know how to do better than any of you." Dudden, to have the advantage of him, jumped in off the bank, and was drowned along with Hudden. And this was the end of Hudden and Dudden.

A Rich Woman

[KATHARINE TYNAN]

Margret Laffan was something of a mystery to the Island people. Long ago in comparative youth she had disappeared for a half-dozen years. Then she had turned up one day in a coarse dress of blue and white check, which looked suspiciously like workhouse or asylum garb, and had greeted such of the neighbours as she knew with a nod, for all the world as if she had seen them yesterday. It happened that the henwife at the Hall had been buried a day or two earlier, and when Margret came asking a place from Mrs. Wilkinson, the lord's housekeeper, the position was yet unfilled and Margret got it.

Not every one would have cared for the post. Only a misanthropic person indeed would have been satisfied with it. The henwife's cottage and the poultry settlement might have been many miles from a human habitation, so lonely were they. They were in a glen of red sandstone, and half the wood lay between them and the Hall. The great red walls stood so high round the glen that you could not even hear the sea calling. As for the village, it was a long way below. You had to go down a steep path from the glen before you came to an open space, where you could see the reek of the chimneys under you. Every morning Margret brought the eggs and the trussed chickens to the Hall. But no one disturbed her solitude, except when the deer, or the wild little red cattle came gazing curiously through the netting at Margret and her charges. There, for twenty-seven years, Margret lived with no company but the fowl. On Sundays and holidays she went to mass to the Island Chapel, but gave no encouragement to those who would have gone a step of the road home with her. The Island women used to wonder how she could bear the loneliness.—"Why, God be betune us and harm!" they often said, "Sure the crathur might be robbed and murdhered any night of the year and no wan the wiser." And so she might, if the Island possessed robbers and murderers in its midst. But it is a primitively innocent little community, which sleeps with open doors as often as not, and there is nothing to tempt marauders or even beggars to migrate there.

By and by a feeling got about that Margret must be saving money. Her wage as a henwife was no great thing, but then, as they said, "she looked as if she lived on the smell of an oil-rag," and there was plenty of food to be had in the Hall kitchen, where Margret waited with her eggs and fowl every morning. Certainly her clothes, though decent, were worn well-nigh threadbare. But the feelers that the neighbours sent out towards Margret met with no solid assurance. Grim and taciturn, Margret kept her own counsel, and was like enough to keep it till the day of her death.

Jack Laffan, Margret's brother, is the village carpenter, a sociable poor man, not the least bit in the world like his sister. Jack is rather fond of idling over a glass with his cronies in the public-house, but, as he is well under Mrs. Jack's thumb, the habit is not likely to grow on him inconveniently. There are four daughters and a son, a lad of fifteen or thereabouts. Two of the daughters are domestic servants out in the big world, and are reported to wear streamers to their caps and fine lace aprons every day. Another is handmaiden to Miss Bell at the post office, and knows the contents of all the letters, except Father Tiernay's, before the people they belong to. Fanny is at home with her father and mother, and is supposed to be too fond of fal-lals, pinchbeck brooches and cheap ribbons, which come to her from her sisters out in the world. She often talks of emigration, and is not sought after by the young men of the Island, who regard her as a "vain paycocky thing."

Mrs. Jack has the reputation of being a hard, managing woman. There was never much love lost between her and Margret, and when the latter came back from her six years' absence on the mainland, Mrs. Jack's were perhaps the most ill-natured surmises as to the reasons for Margret's silence and the meaning of that queer checked garb.

For a quarter of a century Margret lived among her fowl, untroubled by her kin. Then the talk about the money grew from little beginnings like a snowball. It fired Mrs. Jack with a curious excitement, for she was an ignorant woman and ready to believe any extravagant story. She amazed Jack by putting the blame of their long ignoring of Margret upon his shoulders entirely, and when he stared at her, dumbfounded, she seized and shook him till his teeth rattled. "You great stupid omadhaun!" she hissed between the shakes, "that couldn't have the nature in you to see to your own sister, an' she a lone woman!"

That very day Jack went off stupidly to try to bridge over with Margret the gulf of nearly thirty years. He got very little help from his sister. She watched him with what seemed like grim enjoyment while he wriggled miserably on the edge of his chair and tried to talk naturally. At length he

jerked out his wife's invitation to have a bit of dinner with them on the coming Sunday, which Margret accepted without showing any pleasure, and
then he bolted.

Margret came to dinner on the Sunday, and was
well entertained with a fat chicken and a bit of
bacon, for the Laffans were well-to-do people. She
thoroughly enjoyed her dinner, though she spoke little and that little monosyllabic; but Margret was taciturn even as a girl, and her solitary habit for years
seemed to have made speech more difficult for her.
Mrs. Jack heaped her plate with great heartiness and
made quite an honoured guest of her. But outside
enjoying the dinner Margret did not seem to
respond. Young Jack was brought forward to display
his accomplishments, which he did in the most
hang-dog fashion. The cleverness and good-looks
and goodness of the girls were expatiated upon, but
Margret gave no sign of interest. Once Fanny caught
her looking at her with a queer saturnine glance, that
made her feel all at once hot and uncomfortable,
though she had felt pretty secure of her smartness
before that. Margret's reception of Mrs. Jack's over-
tures did not satisfy that enterprising lady. When she
had departed Mrs. Jack put her down as "a flinty-
hearted ould maid." "Her sort," she declared, "is
ever an' always sour an' bitther to them the Lord
blesses wid a family." But all the same it became a

regular thing for Margret to eat her Sunday dinner with the Laffans, and Mrs. Jack discovered after a time that the good dinners were putting a skin and roundness on Margret that might give her a new lease of life—perhaps a not quite desirable result.

The neighbours looked on at Mrs. Jack's "antics" with something little short of scandal. They met by twos and threes to talk over it, and came to the conclusion that Mrs. Jack had no shame at all, at all, in her pursuit of the old woman's money. Truth to tell, there was scarcely a woman in the Island but thought she had as good a right to Margret's money as her newly-attentive kinsfolk. Mrs. Devine and Mrs. Cahill might agree in the morning, with many shakings of the head, that 'Liza Laffan's avarice and greed were beyond measure loathsome. Yet neither seemed pleased to see the other a little later in the day, when Mrs. Cahill climbing the hill with a full basket met Mrs. Devine descending with an empty one.

For all of a sudden a pilgrimage to Margret's cottage in the Red Glen became the recognised thing. It was surprising how old childish friendships and the most distant ties of kindred were furbished up and brought into the light of day. The grass in the lane to the glen became trampled to a regular track. If the women themselves did not come panting up the hill they sent the little girsha, or wee Tommy or Larry, with a little fish, or a griddle cake, or a few fresh greens for Margret. The men of the Island were somewhat scornful of these proceedings on the part of their dames; but as a rule the Island wives hold their own and do pretty well as they will. All this friendship for Margret created curious divisions and many enmities.

Margret, indeed, throve on all the good things, but whether any one person was in her favour more than another it would be impossible to say. Margret got up a way of thanking all alike in a honeyed voice that had a queer sound of mockery in it, and after a time some of the more independent spirits dropped out of the chase, "pitching," as they expressed it, "her ould money to the divil." Mrs. Jack was fairly confident all the time that if any one on the Island got Margret's nest-egg it would be herself, but she had a misgiving which she imparted to her husband that the whole might go to Father Tiernay for charities. Any attempt at getting inside the shell which hid Margret's heart from the world her sister-in-law had long given up. She had also given up trying to interest Margret in "the childher," or bidding young Jack be on his best behaviour before the Sunday guest. The young folk didn't like the derision in Margret's pale eyes, and kept out of her way as much as possible, since they feared their mother too much to flout her openly, as they were often tempted to do.

Two or three years had passed before Margret showed signs of failing. Then at the end of one very cold winter people noticed that she grew feebler. She was away from mass one or two Sundays, and then one Sunday she reappeared walking with the aid of a stick and looking plainly ill and weak. After mass she had a private talk with Father Tiernay at the presbytery; and then went slowly down to Jack's house for the usual dinner. Both Jack and Mrs. Jack saw her home in the afternoon, and a hard task the plucky old woman found it, for all their assistance, to get back to her cottage up the steep hill. When they had reached the top she paused for a rest. Then she said quietly, "I'm thinkin' I'll make no more journeys to the Chapel. Father Tiernay'll have to be coming to me instead."

"Tut, tut, woman dear," said Mrs. Jack, with two hard red spots coming into her cheeks, "we'll be seein' you about finely when the weather gets milder." And then she insinuated in a wheedling voice something about Margret's affairs being settled.

Margret looked up at her with a queer mirthfulness in her glance. "Sure what wud a poor ould woman like me have to settle? Sure that's what they say when a sthrong farmer takes to dyin'."

Mrs. Jack was too fearful of possible consequences to press the matter. She was anxious that Margret should have Fanny to look after the house and the fowl for her, but this Margret refused. "I'll be able to do for myself a little longer," she said, "an' thank you kindly all the same."

When it was known that Margret was failing, the attentions to her became more urgent. Neighbours passed each other now in the lane with a toss of the head and "a wag of the tail." As for Mrs. Jack, who would fain have installed herself altogether in the henwife's cottage, she spent her days quivering with indignation at the meddlesomeness of the other women. She woke Jack up once in the night with a fiery declaration that she'd speak to Father Tiernay about the pursuit of her moneyed relative, but Jack threw cold water on that scheme. "Sure his Riverince himself, small blame to him, 'ud be as glad as another to have the bit. 'Twould be buildin' him the new schoolhouse he's wantin' this many a day, so it would." And this suggestion made Mrs. Jack look askance at her pastor, as being also in the running for the money.

It was surprising how many queer presents found their way to Margret's larder in those days. They who had not the most suitable gift for an invalid brought what they had, and Margret received them all with the same inscrutability. She might have been provisioning for a siege. Mrs. Jack's chickens were flanked by a coarse bit of American bacon; here was a piece of salt ling, there some potatoes in a sack; a slice of salt butter was side by side with a griddle cake. Many a good woman appreciated the waste of good food even while she added to it, and sighed after that full larder for the benefit of her man and the weans at home; but all the time there was the dancing marsh-light of Margret's money luring the good souls on. There had never been any organised robbery in the Island since the cattle-lifting of the kernes long ago; but many a good woman fell of a tremble now when she thought of Margret and her "stocking" alone through the silent night, and at the mercy of midnight robbers.

There was not a day that several offerings were not laid at Margret's feet. But suddenly she changed her stereotyped form of thanks to a mysterious utterance, "You're maybe feeding more than you know, kind neighbours," was the dark saying that set the women conjecturing about Margret's sanity.

Then the bolt fell. One day a big, angular, shambling girl, with Margret's suspicious eyes and cynical mouth, crossed by the ferry to the Island. She had a trunk, which Barney Ryder, general carrier to the Island, would have lifted to his ass-cart, but the newcomer scornfully waved him away. "Come here, you two gorsoons," she said, seizing upon young Jack Laffan and a comrade who were gazing at her grinning, "take a hoult o' the thrunk an' lead the way to Margret Laffan's in the Red Glen. I'll crack sixpence

betune yez when I get there." The lads, full of
curiosity, lifted up the trunk, and preceded her up
the mile or so of hill to Margret's. She stalked after
them into the sunny kitchen where Margret sat
waiting, handed them the sixpence when they had
put down the trunk, bundled them out and shut the
door before she looked towards Margret in her
chimney-corner.

The explanation came first from his Reverence,
who was walking in the evening glow, when Mrs.
Jack Laffan came flying towards him with her cap-
strings streaming.

"Little Jack has a quare story, yer Riverince," she
cried out panting, "about a girl's come visitin' ould
Margret in the glen, an' wid a thrunk as big as a
house. Him an' little Martin was kilt draggin' it up
the hill."

His Reverence waved away her excitement gently.

"I know all about it," he said. "Indeed I've been
the means in a way of restoring Margret's daughter
to her. You never knew your sister-in-law was married, Mrs. Laffan? An odd woman to drop her married name. We must call her by it in future. Mrs.
Conneely is the name."

But Mrs. Jack, with an emotion which even the
presence of his Reverence could not quell, let what
the neighbours described afterwards as a "screech
out of her fit to wake the dead," and fled into her

house, where on her bed she had an attack which came as near being hysterical as the strong-minded woman could compass. She only recovered when Mrs. Devine and Mrs. Cahill and the widow Mulvany, running in, proposed to drench her with cold water, when her heels suddenly left off drumming and she stood up, very determinedly, and bade them be off about their own business. She always spoke afterwards of Margret as the robber of the widow and orphan, which was satisfying if not quite appropriate.

We all heard afterwards how Margret had married on the mainland, and after this girl was born had had an attack of mania, for which she was placed in the county asylum. In time she was declared cured, and it was arranged that her husband should come for her on a certain day and remove her; but Margret, having had enough of marriage and its responsibilities, left the asylum quietly before that day came and made her way to the Island. She had been well content to be regarded as a spinster till she felt her health failing, and then she had entrusted to Father Tiernay her secret, and he had found her daughter for her.

Margret lived some months after that, and left at the time of her death thirty pounds to the fortunate heiress. The well-stocked larder had sufficed the two for quite a long time without any recourse to "the stocking." There was very little further friendship between the village and the Red Glen. Such of the neighbours as were led there at first by curiosity found the door shut in their faces, for Mary had Margret's suspiciousness many times intensified. After the Laffan family had recovered from the first shock of disappointment Fanny made various approaches to her cousin when she met her at mass on the Sundays, and, unheeding rebuffs, sent her a brooch and an apron at Christmas. I wish I could have seen Margret's face and Mary's over that present. It was returned to poor Fanny, with a curt intimation that Mary had no use for it, and there the matter ended.

I once asked Mary, when I knew her well enough to take the liberty, about that meeting between her and her mother, after the door was shut on young Jack's and little Martin's departing footsteps. "Well," said Mary, "she looked hard at me, an' then she said, 'You've grown up yalla an' badlookin', but a strong girl for the work. You favour meself, though I've a genteeler nose.' And then," said Mary, "I turned in an' boiled the kettle for the tay."

The money did not even remain in the Island, for as soon as Margret was laid in a grave in the Abbey—with a vacant space beside her, for, said Mary, "you couldn't tell but I'd be takin' a fancy to be buried there myself some day,"—Mary fled in the early morning before the neighbours were about. Mary looked on the Island where so many had coveted her money as a "nest of robbers," and so she fled, with "the stocking" in the bosom of her gown, one morning at low tide. She wouldn't trust the money to the post office in the Island, because her cousin Lizzie was Miss Bell's servant. "Divil a letther but the priest's they don't open an' read," she said, "an' tells the news afterwards to the man or woman that owns it. The news gets to them before the letter. An' if I put the fortune in there I'm doubtin' 'twould ever see London. I know an honest man in the Whiterock post office I'd betther be trustin."

And that is how Margret's "stocking" left the Island.

Penelope's Irish Experiences

$\mathcal{C}\!\!\!\!\sim$

[KATE DOUGLAS WIGGIN]

CHAPTER I

The light-hearted daughters of Erin,
Like the wild mountain deer they can bound;
Their feet never touch the green island,
But music is struck from the ground.
And oft in the glens and green meadows,
The ould jig they dance with such grace,
That even the daisies they tread on,
Look up with delight in their face.

—*James M'Kowen*

One of our favorite diversions is an occasional glimpse of a "crossroads dance" on a pleasant Sunday afternoon, when all the young people of the district are gathered together. Their religious duties are over with their confessions and their masses, and the priests encourage these decorous Sabbath gayeties. A place is generally chosen where two or four roads meet, and the dancers come from the scattered farmhouses in every direction. In Ballyfuchsia, they dance on a flat piece of road under some fir-trees and larches, with stretches of mountain covered with yellow gorse or purple heather and the quiet lakes lying in the distance. A message comes down to use at Ardnagreena—where we commonly spend our Sunday afternoons—that they expect a good dance, and the blind boy is coming to fiddle; and "so if you will be coming up, it's welcome you'll be." We join them about five o'clock—passing, on our way, groups of "boys" of all ages from sixteen upwards, walking in twos and threes, and parties of three or four girls by themselves; for it would not be etiquette for the boys and girls to walk together, such strictness is observed in these matters about here.

When we reach the rendezvous we find quite a crowd of young men and maidens assembled; the girls all at one side of the road, neatly dressed in dark skirts and light blouses, with the national woolen shawl over their heads. Two wide stone walls, or dikes, with turf on top, make capital seats, and the boys are at the opposite side, as custom demands. When a young man wants a partner, he steps across the road and asks a colleen, who lays

aside her shawl, generally giving it to a younger sister to keep until the dance is over, when the girls go
back to their own side of the road and put on their
shawls again. Upon our arrival we find the "sets"
are already in progress; a "set" being a dance like a
very intricate and very long quadrille. We are
greeted with many friendly words, and the young
boatmen and farmers' sons ask the ladies, "Will you
be pleased to dance, miss?" Some of them are shy,
and say they are not familiar with the steps; but their
would-be partners remark encouragingly: "Sure,
and what matter? I'll see you through." Soon all are
dancing, and the state of the road is being discussed
with as much interest as the floor of a ballroom.
Eager directions are given to the more ignorant
newcomers, such as, "Twirl your girl, captain!" or
"Turn your back to your face!"—rather a difficult
direction to carry out, but one which conveys its
meaning. Salemina confided to her partner that she
feared she was getting a bit old to dance. He looked
at her gray hair carefully for a moment, and then
said chivalrously: "I'd not say that that was old age,
ma'am. I'd say it was eddication."

When the sets, which are very long and very
decorous, are finished, sometimes a jig is danced for
our benefit. The spectators make a ring, and the
chosen dancers go into the middle, where their steps
are watched by a most critical and discriminating

audience with the most minute and intense interest. Our Molly is one of the best jig dancers among the girls here (would that she were half as clever at cooking!); but if you want to see an artist of the first rank, you must watch Kitty O'Rourke, from the neighboring village of Dooclone. The half door of the barn is carried into the ring by one or two of her admirers, whom she numbers by the score, and on this she dances her famous jig polthogue, sometimes alone and sometimes with Art Rooney, the only worthy partner for her in the kingdom of Kerry. Art's mother, "Bid" Rooney, is a keen matchmaker, and we heard her the other day advising her son, who was going to Dooclone to have a "weeny court" with his colleen, to put a clane shirt on him in the middle of the week, and disthract Kitty intirely by showin' her he had three of thim, annyway!

Kitty is a beauty, and does n't need to be made "purty wid cows"—a feat that the old Irishman proposed to do when he was consummating a match for his plain daughter. But the gifts of the gods seldom come singly, and Kitty is well fortuned as well as beautiful; fifty pounds, her own bedstead and its fittings, a cow, a pig, and a web of linen are supposed to be the dazzling total, so that it is small wonder her deluderin' ways are maddening half the boys in Ballyfuchsia and Dooclone. She has the prettiest pair of feet in the County Kerry, and when they are encased in a smart pair of shoes, bought for her by Art's rival, the big constable from Ballyfuchsia barracks, how they do twinkle and caper over that half barn door, to be sure! Even Murty, the blind fiddler, seems intoxicated by the plaudits of the bystanders, and he certainly never plays so well for anybody as for Kitty of the Meadow. Blindness is still common in Ireland, owing to the smoke in these wretched cabins, where sometimes a hole in the roof is the only chimney; and although the scores of blind fiddlers no longer traverse the land, finding a welcome at all firesides, they are still to be found in every community. Blind Murty is a favorite guest at the Rooney's cabin, which is never so full that there is not room for one more. There is a small wooden bed in the main room, a settle that opens out at night, with hens in the straw underneath, where a board keeps them safely within until they have finished laying. There are six children besides Art, and my ambition is to photograph; or, still better, to sketch the family circle together; the hens cackling under the settle, the pig ("him as pays the rint") snoring in the doorway, as a proprietor should, while the children are pic-turesquely grouped about. I never succeed, because Mrs. Rooney sees us as we turn into the lane, and calls to the family to make itself ready, as quality's comin' in sight. The older children can scramble under the bed, slip shoes over their bare feet, and be out in front of the cabin without the loss of a single minute. "Mickey jew'l," the baby, who is only four, but "who can handle a stick as bould as a man," is generally clad in a ragged skirt, slit every few inches from waist to hem, so that it resembles a cotton fringe. The little coateen that tops this costume is sometimes, by way of diversion, transferred to the dog, who runs off with it; but if we appear at this unlucky moment, there is a stylish yoke of pink ribbon and soiled lace which one of the girls pins over Mickey jew'l's naked shoulders.

Moya, who has this eye for picturesque propriety, is a great friend of mine, and has many questions about the Big Country when we take our walks. She longs to emigrate, but the time is not ripe yet. "The girls that come back has a lovely style to thim," she says wistfully, "but they're so polite they can't live in the cabins anny more and be contint." The "boys" are not always so improved, she thinks. "You'd niver find a boy in Ballyfuchsia that would say annything rude to a girl; but when they come back from Ameriky, it's too free they've grown intirely." It is a dull life for them, she says, when they have once been away; though to be sure Ballyfuchsia is a pleasanter place than Dooclone, where the priest does not approve of dancing, and, however secretly you may do it, the curate hears of it, and will speak your name in church.

It was Moya who told me of Kitty's fortune. "She 's not the match that Farmer Brodigan's daughter Kathleen is, to be sure; for he 's a rich man, and has given her an iligant eddication in Cork, so that she can look high for a husband. She won't be takin' up wid anny of our boys, wid her two hundred pounds and her twenty cows and her pianya. Och, it 's a thriminjus player she is, ma'am. She 's that quick and that strong that you 'd say she would n't lave a string on it."

Some of the young men and girls never see each other before the marriage, Moya says. "But sure," she adds shyly, "I'd niver be contint with that, though some love matches does n't turn out anny better than the others."

"I hope it will be a love match with you, and that I shall dance at your wedding, Moya," I say to her smilingly.

"Faith, I 'm thinkin' my husband's intinded mother died an old maid in Dublin," she answers merrily. "It 's a small fortune I 'll be havin', and few lovers; but you 'll be soon dancing at Kathleen Brodigan's wedding, or Kitty O'Rourke's, maybe."

I do not pretend to understand these humble romances, with their foundations of cows and linen, which are after all no more sordid than bank stock and trousseaux from Paris. The sentiment of the Irish peasant lover seems to be frankly and truly expressed in the verses:—

"Oh! Moya's wise and beautiful, has wealth in
plenteous store,
And fortune fine in calves and kine, and lovers
half a score;
Her faintest smile would saints beguile, or sin-
ners captivate,
Oh! I think a dale of Moya, but I'll surely
marry Kate.

Now to let you know the raison why I cannot
have my way,
Nor bid my heart decide the part the lover
must obey—
The calves and kine of Kate are nine, while
Moya owns but eight,
So with all my love for Moya I'm compelled
to marry Kate!"

I gave Moya a lace neckerchief the other day, and
she was rarely pleased, running into the cabin with it
and showing it to her mother with great pride. After
we had walked a bit down the boreen she excused
herself for an instant, and, returning to my side,
explained that she had gone back to ask her mother
to mind the kerchief, and not let the "cow knock it"!

Lady Killbally tells us that some of the girls who
work in the mills deny themselves proper food, and
live on bread and tea for a month, to save the price

of a gay ribbon. This is trying, no doubt, to a phi-
lanthropist, but is it not partly a starved sense of
beauty asserting itself? If it has none of the usual
outlets, where can imagination express itself if not in
some paltry thing like a ribbon?

CHAPTER II

In Ould Donegal

Here 's a health to you, Father O'Flynn!
Slainté, and slainté, and slainté agin;
Pow'rfulest preacher and tenderest teacher,
And kindliest creature in ould Donegal.

—*Alfred Perceval Graves*

It is a far cry from the kingdom of Kerry to "ould
Donegal," where we have been traveling for a week,
chiefly in the hope of meeting Father O'Flynn. We
miss our careless, genial, ragged, southern Paddy just
a bit; for he was a picturesque, likable figure, on the
whole, and easier to know than this Ulster Irishman,
the product of a mixed descent.

We did not stop long in Belfast; for if there is anything we detest, when on our journeys, it is to mix
too much with people of industry, thrift, and business sagacity. Sturdy, prosperous, calculating, well-to-
do Protestants are well enough in their way, and

undoubtedly they make a very good backbone for Ireland; but we crave something more romantic than the citizen virtues, or we should have remained in our own country, where they are tolerably common, although we have not as yet anything approaching overproduction.

Belfast, it seems, is and has always been, a centre of Presbyterianism. The members of the Presbytery protested against the execution of Charles I., and received an irate reply from Milton, who said that "the blockish presbyters of Claudeboy" were "egregious liars and impostors," who meant to stir up rebellion "from their unchristian synagogue at Belfast in a barbarous nook of Ireland."

Ireland is no longer a battlefield of English parties, neither is it wholly a laboratory for political experiment; but from having been both the one and the other, its features are a bit knocked out of shape and proportion, as it were. We have bought two hideous engravings of The Battle of the Boyne and The Secret of England's Greatness; and whenever we stay for a night in any inn where perchance these are not, we pin them on the wall, and are received into the landlady's heart at once. I don't know which is the finer study: the picture of his Majesty William III crossing the Boyne, or the plump little Queen presenting a huge family Bible to an apparently uninterested black youth. In the latter work of art the eye is confused at first as the three principal features approach each other very nearly in size, and Francesca asked innocently, "Which *is* the secret of England's greatness—the Bible, the Queen, or the black man?"

This is a thriving town, and we are at a smart hotel which had for two years an English manager. The scent of the roses hangs round it still, but it is gradually growing fainter under the stress of small patronage and other adverse circumstances. The table linen is a trifle ragged, though clean; but the circle of red and green wineglasses by each plate, an array not borne out by the number of vintages on the wine list, the tiny ferns scattered everywhere in innumerable pots, and the dozens of minute glass vases, each holding a few blue hyacinths, give an air of urban elegance to the dining-room. The guests are requested in printed placards to be punctual at meals, especially at the seven-thirty *table d'hôte* dinner, and the management itself is punctual at this function about seven forty-five. This is much better than at the south, where we, and sixty other travelers, were once kept waiting fifteen minutes between the soup and the fish course. When we were finally served with half-cooked turbot, a pleasant-spoken waitress went about to each table, explaining to the irate guests that the cook was "not at her best." We caught a glimpse of her as she was being borne aloft, struggling and eloquent, and were able to understand the reason of her unachieved ideals.

There is nothing sacred about dinner to the average Irishman; he is willing to take anything that comes, as a rule, and cooking is not regarded as a fine art here. Perhaps occasional flashes of starvation and seasons of famine have rendered the Irish palate easier to please; at all events, wherever the national god may be, its pedestal is not in the stomach. Our breakfast, day after day, week after week, has been bacon and eggs. One morning we had tomatoes on bacon, and concluded that the cook had experienced religion or fallen in love, since both these operations send a flush of blood to the brain and stimulate the mental processes. But no; we found simply that the eggs had not been brought in time for breakfast. There is no consciousness of monotony—far from it; the nobility and gentry can at least eat what they choose, and they choose bacon and eggs. There is no running of the family gamut, either, from plain boiled to omelet; poached or fried eggs on bacon, it is, week days and Sundays. The luncheon, too, is rarely inspired: they eat cold joint of beef with pickled beet root, or mutton and boiled potatoes, with unfailing regularity, finishing off at most hotels with semolina pudding, a concoction intended for, and appealing solely to, the taste of the toothless infant, who, having just graduated from rubber rings, has not a jaded palate.

How the long breakfast bill at an up-to-date Belfast hostelry awed us, after weeks of bacon and eggs! The viands on the menu swam together before our dazed eyes.

> Porridge
>
> Fillets of Plaice
>
> Whiting
>
> Fried Sole
>
> Savoury Omelet
>
> Kidneys and Bacon
>
> Cold Meats

I looked at this array like one in a dream, realizing that I had lost the power of selection, and remembering the scientific fact that unused faculties perish for want of exercise. The man who was serving us rattled his tray, shifted his weight wearily from one foot to the other and cleared his throat suggestively; until at last I said hastily, "Bacon and eggs, please," and Salemina, the most critical person in the party, murmured, "The same."

Oisin and Patrick

[LADY GREGORY]

As to Oisin, it was a long time after he was brought away by Niamh that he came back again to Ireland. Some say it was hundreds of years he was in the Country of the Young, and some say it was thousands of years he was in it; but whatever time it was, it seemed short to him.

And whatever happened him through the time he was away, it is a withered old man he was found after coming back to Ireland, and his white horse going away from him, and he lying on the ground.

And it was S. Patrick had power at that time, and it was to him Oisin was brought; and he kept him in his house, and used to be teaching him and questioning him. And Oisin was no way pleased with the way Ireland was then, but he used to be talking of the old times, and fretting after the Fianna.

And Patrick bade him to tell what happened him the time he left Finn and the Fianna and went away with Niamh. And it is the story Oisin told:—"The time I went away with golden-haired Niamh, we turned our backs to the land, and our faces westward, and the sea was going away before us, and filling up in waves after us. And we saw wonderful things on our journey," he said, "cities and courts and duns and lime-white houses, and shining sunny-houses and palaces. And one time we saw beside us a hornless deer running hard, and an eager white red-eared hound following after it. And another time we saw a young girl on a horse and having a golden apple in her right hand, and she going over the tops of the waves; and there was following after her a young man riding a white horse, and having a crimson cloak and a gold-hilted sword in his right hand."

"Follow on with your story, pleasant Oisin," said Patrick, "for you did not tell us yet what was the country you went to."

"The Country of the Young, the Country of Victory, it was," said Oisin. "And O Patrick," he said, "there is no lie in that name; and if there are grandeurs in your Heaven the same as there are there, I would give my friendship to God.

"We turned our backs then to the dun," he said, "and the horse under us was quicker than the spring wind on the backs of the mountains. And it was not long till the sky darkened, and the wind rose in every part, and the sea was as if on fire, and there was nothing to be seen of the sun.

"But after we were looking at the clouds and the stars for a while the wind went down, and the storm, and the sun brightened. And we saw before us a very delightful country under full blossom, and smooth plains in it, and a king's dun that was very grand, and that had every colour in it, and sunny-houses beside it, and palaces of shining stones, made by skilled men. And we saw coming out to meet us three fifties of armed men, very lively and handsome. And I asked Niamh was this the Country of the Young, and she said it was. 'And indeed, Oisin,' she said, 'I told you no lie about it, and you will see all I promised you before you for ever.'

"And there came out after that a hundred beautiful young girls, having cloaks of silk worked with gold, and they gave me a welcome to their own country. And after that there came a great shining army, and with it a strong beautiful king, having a shirt of yellow silk and a golden cloak over it, and a very bright crown on his head. And there was following after him a young queen, and fifty young girls along with her.

"And when all were come to the one spot, the king took me by the hand, and he said out before them all: 'A hundred thousand welcomes before you,

Oisin, son of Finn. And as to this country you are come to,' he said, 'I will tell you news of it without a lie. It is long and lasting your life will be in it, and you yourself will be young for ever. And there is no delight the heart ever thought of,' he said, 'but it is here against your coming. And you can believe my words, Oisin,' he said, 'for I myself am the King of the Country of the Young, and this is its comely queen, and it was golden-headed Niamh our daughter that went over the sea looking for you to be her husband for ever.' I gave thanks to him then, and I stooped myself down before the queen, and we went forward to the royal house, and all the high nobles came out to meet us, both men and women, and there was a great feast made there through the length of ten days and ten nights.

"And that is the way I married Niamh of the Golden Hair, and that is the way I went to the Country of the Young, although it is sorrowful to me to be telling it now, O Patrick from Rome," said Oisin.

"Follow on with your story, Oisin of the destroying arms," said Patrick, "and tell me what way did you leave the Country of the Young, for it is long to me till I hear that; and tell us now had you any children by Niamh, and was it long you were in that place."

"Two beautiful children I had by Niamh," said Oisin, "two young sons and a comely daughter.

And Niamh gave the two sons the name of Finn and of Osgar, and the name I gave to the daughter was The Flower.

"And I did not feel the time passing, and it was a long time I stopped there," he said, "till the desire came on me to see Finn and my comrades again. And I asked leave of the king and of Niamh to go back to Ireland. 'You will get leave from me,' said Niamh; 'but for all that,' she said, 'it is bad news you are giving me, for I am in dread you will never come back here again through the length of your days.' But I bade her have no fear, since the white horse would bring me safe back again from Ireland. 'Bear this in mind, Oisin,' she said then, 'if you once get off the horse while you are away, or if you once put your foot to ground, you will never come back here again. And O Oisin,' she said, 'I tell it to you now for the third time, if you once get down from the horse, you will be an old man, blind and withered, without liveliness, without mirth, without running, without leaping. And it is a grief to me, Oisin,' she said, 'you ever to go back to green Ireland; and it is not now as it used to be, and you will not see Finn and his people, for there is not now in the whole of Ireland but a Father of Orders and armies of saints; and here is my kiss for you, pleasant Oisin,' she said, 'for you will never come back any more to the Country of the Young.'

"And that is my story, Patrick, and I have told you no lie in it," said Oisin. "And O Patrick," he said, "if I was the same the day I came here as I was that day, I would have made an end of all your clerks, and there would not be a head left on a neck after me."

"Go on with your story," said Patrick, "and you will get the same good treatment from me you got from Finn, for the sound of your voice is pleasing to me."

So Oisin went on with his story, and it is what he said: "I have nothing to tell of my journey till I came back into green Ireland, and I looked about me then on all sides, but there were no tidings to be got of Finn. And it was not long till I saw a great troop of riders, men and women, coming towards me from the west. And when they came near they wished me good health; and there was wonder on them all when they looked at me, seeing me so unlike themselves, and so big and so tall.

"I asked them then did they hear if Finn was still living, or any other one of the Fianna, or what had happened them. 'We often heard of Finn that lived long ago,' said they, 'and that there never was his equal for strength or bravery or a great name; and there is many a book written down,' they said, 'by the sweet poets of the Gael, about his doings and the doings of the Fianna, and it would be hard for us to tell you all of them. And we heard Finn had a son,' they said, 'that was beautiful and shining, and that there came a young girl looking for him, and he went away with her to the Country of the Young.'

"And when I knew by their talk that Finn was not living or any of the Fianna, it is downhearted I was, and tired, and very sorrowful after them. And I made no delay, but I turned my face and went on to Almhuin of Leinster. And there was great wonder on me when I came there to see no sign at all of Finn's great dun, and his great hall, and nothing in the place where it was but weeds and nettles."

And there was grief on Oisin then, and he said: "Och, Patrick! Och, ochone, my grief! It is a bad journey that was to me; and to be without tidings of Finn or the Fianna has left me under pain through my lifetime."

"Leave off fretting, Oisin," said Patrick, "and shed your tears to the God of grace. Finn and the Fianna are slack enough now, and they will get no help for ever." "It is a great pity that would be," said Oisin, "Finn to be in pain for ever; and who was it gained the victory over him, when his own hand had made an end of so many a hard fighter?"

"It is God gained the victory over Finn," said Patrick, "and not the strong hand of an enemy; and as to the Fianna, they are condemned to hell along with him, and tormented for ever."

"O Patrick," said Oisin, "show me the place where Finn and his people are, and there is not a hell or a heaven there but I will put it down. And if Osgar, my own son, is there," he said, "the hero that was bravest in heavy battles, there is not in hell or in the Heaven of God a troop so great that he could not destroy it."

"Let us leave off quarrelling on each side now," said Patrick; "and go on, Oisin, with your story. What happened you after you knew the Fianna to be at an end?"

"I will tell you that, Patrick," said Oisin. "I was turning to go away, and I saw the stone trough that the Fianna used to be putting their hands in, and it full of water. And when I saw it I has such a wish and such a feeling for it that I forgot what I was told, and I got off the horse. And in the minute all the years came on me, and I was lying on the ground, and the horse took fright and went away and left me there, an old man, weak and spent, without sight, without shape, without comeliness, without strength or understanding, without respect.

"There, Patrick, is my story for you now," said Oisin, "and no lie in it, of all that happened me going away and coming back again from the Country of the Young."

The Gaelic Concert

[ELLIS N. MYLES]

"I saw by a poster up at the station that there will be a Gaelic concert on Sunday in Ballyholt, in aid of the new Gaelic College which is to be opened next month," said Eileen O'Hara to Miss O'Connor, with whom she was spending her vacation.

Eileen was from Dublin, and being a very enthusiastic Gaelic Leaguer had come down to Cillesenan in order to practice her Irish with Miss O'Connor, who was a great Gaelic scholar and niece of a famous novelist.

Miss O'Connor had worried the authorities until they had changed the name of the station from English to Irish. She had also done her best to bring Irish manufactures to the notice of the "Shoneen" population of Cillesenan by occasionally holding a small exhibition of Irish-made jellies, jams, biscuits, mineral waters, chemicals, etc.

Cillesenan is a very fashionable watering place patronized chiefly by the would-be English from Rathmines and other British strongholds; so that it was something of a feat to have had the station name put up in Irish. (This was, of course, in the early days of the Gaelic League.)

Ballyholt, which is seven miles from Cillesenan, is an Irish-speaking district, though like many another Irish-speaking district, the priests and schoolteachers spoke nothing but English and favored English sports, songs and music.

A travelling Gaelic League teacher had been appointed for the villages and townlands around Cillesenan, and each night he cycled to one or other of the places to teach Irish.

Miss O'Connor met the teacher a day or two after Eileen had told her about the Gaelic concert and asked him if he were going to Ballyholt on the following Sunday.

"Well," he replied. "I should like to go, but I am afraid I shall get into Father Collins' bad books, as there has been some little trouble over this same concert. Father Murphy, the curate, had the advertising matter printed at the Unionist printers instead of at the Nationalist firm, and Father Collins has told the singers and dancers not to go, so I don't know what to do."

"Well, Sean," said Miss O'Connor, "I think you ought to go. It would look very bad for the Gaelic teacher to stay away from the Gaelic concert. You had better come with us and the 'Eire Og' children. We are hiring Dunne's wagonette, and there will be plenty of room for you."

"Very well, Miss O'Connor, I'll go along with you. I must be pushing on to the mountain now, so slan leat."

Sunday afternoon was very stormy, and soon after Miss O'Connor's party started out to Ballyholt the rain teemed down and they were nearly drowned in the seven Irish miles' drive.

When they arrived at Ballyholt Father Murphy (known among his parishioners as "the crame colored curate," as he drove a cream colored pony and trap, and he was very fair-haired) came out to greet them, and said in English: "Welcome!"— although he knew they were the Gaelic representatives from Cillesenan. They descended from the wagonette and made their way to the already crowded schoolroom.

The schoolroom stood a little below the level of the ground and there were three or four steps leading down to it.

Most of the seats were taken except a few in the front, which were reserved for the aristocracy of Ballyholt, such as the Protestant doctor and family and the district inspector of police and family. Seats could not be found for all the people and they stood up at the back, packed like sardines in a box, whilst there were some who could not get in at all—at least their heads came over the jamb of the door, and the rest of their bodies were outside on the steps.

The concert was very late in commencing, and the audience was becoming restive, and those standing at the back swayed backwards and forwards like the waves of the sea. The din of conversation rose higher and higher, and more commotion was made by a man going round and asking the people to get up from their seats while he lighted a number of oil lamps hanging on the wall and down the middle of the room. This performance took up half the evening, and the other half was taken up with turning them down, as they were smoking.

Father Murphy shouted at the boys to keep quiet several times and threatened to turn them out.

Most of the artistes stayed away on account of Father Collins' order, and performers had to be obtained from other sources.

Just before the concert started Father Murphy discovered there were only three dancers for the four hand reel, and not another could be found. He then remembered that Miss O'Connor had introduced Eileen O'Hara as being from the Dublin Gaelic League, and he went around to ask her to help them out of their difficulty by making up the set for the four hand reel. Eileen demurred at first, as she knew they danced it differently there to what it was danced in Dublin, but after a while she was persuaded to do so.

Well, at last the concert commenced. The first item on the program was a piano solo by the "National" schoolteacher, Miss Higgins, who was dressed in a white dress with a blue sash and wore a red rose in her hair. A little boy about four years old behind Eileen proclaimed in a loud voice: "I would not wear England's bloody red, so I would not." His mother's shocked remarks were drowned by the loud clashing chords of a selection of English airs which included "Rule Britannia." The audience did not applaud this musical performance, but were chatting audibly, shunting chairs about, and Father Murphy had to shout, "Order!"

The second item was a song by a young man about the "Handy Man" of the British Navy. A few claps from the doctors' and district inspectors' families in the front rows followed this song.

Miss Baird, the doctor's daughter, then rendered "A May Madrigal" in a high-pitched, squeaky, shaky voice. Out of respect to the doctor, she was applauded, but not vociferously.

Old Mike Regan, the next to appear, was one of the "star" turns of the evening. He was the village wag and "playboy," and when he appeared on the platform he was greeted with loud cheers. He brought his elder brother with him to accompany him on the whistle.

After a few bows to the cheering audience Mike started his jig evolutions—"leps," the neighbors called them. He sprang up in the air after the manner of a rubber ball and came down again on the platform with a bang. He repeated the "leps" several times, then bowed. His marvelous "step dancing" evoked loud applause—clapping of hands and cries of "Up Ballyholt!" "Good man, Mike!" "Aris!" came from all parts of the room. To the cries of "Aris" (encore) Mike merely shook his head, as he was quite out of breath, and clumsily descended from the platform.

The veteran Mike was followed by a young shop assistant who was down from Limerick on his vacation. To the surprise of everyone he sang a most vulgar and objectionable English music hall song—"Lanigan, Take Me to the Isle of Man Again." As he was a stranger he was given some applause merely because he was a stranger, and not on account of any merit in the song or the singer.

Miss Higgins then gave the "Irish Emigrant."

At last we came to the Gaelic part of the concert—"An madar in ruadh," ["The Fox"] by Sean O'Donoghue, the Gaelic League teacher, was announced, and at the end the first real applause was given, and cries of "Aris!" "Go mait, a buacaill!" ["Good man!"] were heard on all sides except the front seats of the aristocracy. The applause continued until Sean started up with "An ros geal dubh."

After Sean's song there was a short interval, and the room buzzed with Irish conversation. It seemed that the hearing of the beautiful Gaelic words of the songs had unscrewed the valves that had been tightened up during the English items. Here and there a few sentences in English were heard, but bi an Gaedilg ar an mbarr.

Father Murphy fussed over to Eileen O'Hara and brought her to the platform, which she mounted in great trepidation and made her debut as a dancer— her first and last appearance in public.

The platform was rigged up on four empty barrels—one at each corner, and every step that was danced shook the whole construction, and poor Eileen thought every minute that she would fall through the boards. She managed to get through the reel, although, as she had suspected, they danced it somewhat differently to what they did in Dublin. The reel was also well applauded.

The young man from Limerick once more took the platform and gave two of Harry Lauder's songs—"Jean, Jean From Aberdeen," and "Ma Scotch Bluebell."

Miss Higgins, the "National" schoolteacher, gave another display of her English pianoforte solos—there was another "step dancing" or "lepping" turn by old Mike Regan and a duet by Maire McNamara and Sean O'Donoghue, and the concert proper finished: but now the great event of the evening was to take place. Father Murphy announced that they would hear something wonderful if they would "only keep quiet. . . . You will hear the great Italian singer, Signor Caruso." The swaying to and fro of the multitude who were standing at the back and the hum of whispered comments began, and Father Murphy became annoyed and said: "You are going to hear for sixpence (12 cents) what Caruso was paid £200 a night for singing, and if you do not keep quiet, I'll turn you all out without hearing it."

At long last silence was obtained, and Father Murphy after fixing the gramophone up on the platform pulled out a record and adjusted it to the machine. To his horror and the delight of the audience (except the front rows) the first bars of the "Boys of Wexford" gurgled out in a scratchy effort to get free. The boys at the back began to whistle the air. Father Murphy snatched off the offending record—this was a terrible rebel song for the doctor and the district inspector to hear, and whatever would they think of Father Murphy having such a record. After some searching he found the celebrated Caruso's song and put it on. Meantime the crowd at the back—especially those unfortunates with their heads over the top of the open door—had again become very restive and fidgety, and once more Father Murphy had to shout "Order!"

Well, Caruso at last "got under way," but the first sounds that issued were something between a cough and a cat's sneeze. The boys thought this great sport and laughed loudly, nearly driving the already overwrought priest mad. Eventually the record was readjusted and this time "La donna e mobile" in Italian was rendered by the great tenor. The occupants of the front rows were most enthusiastic—since they were so well versed in Italian opera (perhaps), but the rest of the people did not seem to appreciate Italian singing—a good song in Gaelic was much more to their taste.

Caruso's Italian song finished the Gaelic concert, and the boys and girls tumbled noisily out—glad to be out of the hot, packed room—commenting on the various artistes, and feeling disappointed over the "Gaelic" concert—especially Eileen O'Hara, who had expected to hear some of the good old Irish songs that were not usually heard in the Gaelic League.

All the Cillesenan crowd returned home wet through and feeling very dejected, and wished they had stayed away.

Since those days the Irish College at Ballyholt has flourished and grown and the students often give good and really Gaelic concerts and plays, and the people of Ballyholt have awakened to the importance of their native language, songs and dances, and all the Irish speakers are very glad to help those attending the college in every way they can. An Gaedilg abu!

The Battle of the Berrins

[SAMUEL LOVER]

I was sitting alone in the desolate church-yard of ——, intent upon my "silent art," lifting up my eyes from my portfolio, only to direct them to the interesting ruin I was sketching—when the deathlike stillness that prevailed was broken by a faint and wild sound, unlike any thing I had ever heard in my life. I confess I was startled—I paused in my occupation, and listened in breathless expectation. Again this seemingly unearthly sound vibrated through the still air of evening, more audibly than at first, and partaking of the vibratory quality of tone I have noticed, in so great a degree as to resemble the remote sound of the ringing of many glasses crowded together.

I rose and looked around—no being was near me, and again this heart-chilling sound struck upon my ear; its wild and wailing intonation reminding me of the Æolian harp. Another burst was wafted up the hill; and then it became discernible that the sound proceeded from many voices raised in lamentation.

It was the *ulican*. I had hitherto known it only by report; for the first time, now, its wild and appalling cadence had ever been heard; and it will not be wondered at by those acquainted with it that I was startled on hearing it under such circumstances.

I could now perceive a crowd of peasants of both sexes, winding along a hollow way that led to the church-yard where I was standing, bearing amongst them the coffin of the departed; and ever and anon a wild burst of the *ulican* would arise from the throng, and ring in wild startling *unison* up the hill until, by a gradual and plaintive descent through an *octave,* it dropped into a subdued wail; and they bore the body onward the while, not in the measured and solemn step that custom (at least our custom) deems decent, but in a rapid and irregular manner, as if the violence of their grief hurried them on, and disdained all form.

The effect was certainly more impressive than that of any other funeral I had ever witnessed, however much the "pride, pomp, and circumstance," of such arrays had been called upon to produce a studied solemnity; for no hearse with sable plumes, nor chief mourners, nor pall-bearers, ever equalled in *poetry* or *picturesque* these poor people, bearing along on their shoulders, in the stillness of evening, the body of their departed friend to its "long home." The women raising their arms above their heads, in the untaught action of grief; their dark and ample cloaks waving wildly about, agitated by the varied motions of their wearers, and their wild cry raised in lament

"Most musical, most melancholy."

At length they reached the cemetery, and the coffin was borne into the interior of the ruin, where the women still continued to wail for the dead, while half a dozen athletic young men immediately proceeded to prepare a grave; and seldom have I seen finer fellows, or men more full of activity; their action, indeed, bespoke so much life and vigour, as to induce an involuntary and melancholy contrast with the object on which that action was bestowed.

Scarcely had the spade upturned the green sod of the burial-ground, when the wild peal of the *ulican* again was heard at a distance. The young men paused in their work, and turned their heads, as did all the bystanders, towards the point whence the sound proceeded.

We soon perceived another funeral procession wind round the foot of the hill, and immediately the gravemakers renewed their work with redoubled activity; while exclamations of anxiety on their part, for the completion of their work, and of encouragement from the lookers-on, resounded on all sides; and such ejaculations as "Hurry, boys, hurry!"—"Sir yourself, Paddy!"—"That's your sort, Mike!"—"Rouse, your sowl!" &c., &c., resounded on all sides. At the same time, the second funeral party that was advancing, no sooner perceived the church-yard already occupied, then they directly quickened their pace, as the wail rose more loudly and wildly from the train; and a detachment bearing pick and spade, forthwith sallied from the main body, and dashed with headlong speed up the hill. In the mean time, an old woman, with streaming eyes and dishevelled hair, rushed wildly from the ruin where the first party had borne their coffin, towards the young athletes I have already described as working with "might and main," and addressing them with all the passionate intensity of her country, she exclaimed, "Sure you wouldn't let them have the advantage of uz, that-a-way, and lave my darlin' boy wanderhin' about, dark an' 'lone in the long nights. Work, boys! work! for the bare life, and the mother's blessing be an you, and let my poor Paudeen have rest."

I thought the poor woman was crazed, as indeed her appearance and vehemence of manner, as well as the (to me) unintelligible address she had uttered, might well induce me to believe, and I questioned one of the bystanders accordingly.

"An' is it why she's goin' wild about it, you're axin'?" said the person I addressed, in evident wonder at my question. "Sure then I thought all the world know that, let alone a gintleman like you, that ought to be knowledgable: and sure she doesn't want the poor boy to be walkin', as of coorse he must, barrin' they're smart."

"What do you mean?" said I, "I don't understand you."

"Whisht! whisht," said he; "here they come, by the powers, and the Gallaghers at the head of them," as he looked towards the new-comers' advanced-guard, who had now gained the summit of the hill, and, leaping over the boundary-ditch of the cemetery, advanced towards the group that surrounded the grave, with rapid strides and a resolute air.

"Giv over there, I bid you," said a tall and ably-built man of the party, to those employed in opening the ground, who still plied their implements with energy.

"Give over, or it 'll be worse for you. Didn't you hear me, Rooney?" said he, as he laid his muscular hand on the arm of one of the party he addressed, and arrested him in his occupation.

"I did hear you," said Rooney; "but I didn't heed you."

"I'd have you keep a civil tongue in your head," said the former.

"You're mighty ready to give advice that you want yourself," rejoined the latter, as he again plunged the spade into the earth.

"Lave off, I tell you!" said our Hercules, in a higher tone; "or, by this and that, I'll make you sorry!"

"Arrah! what brings you here at all?" said another of the grave-makers, "breedin' a disturbance?"

"What brings him here but mischief?" said a grey-haired man, who undertook, with national peculiarity, to answer one interrogatory by making another—"there's always a quarrel, whenever there's a Gallagher." For it was indeed one of "the Gallaghers" that the peasant I spoke to noticed as being "at the head o' them," who was assuming so bold a tone.

"You may thank your grey hairs, that I don't make you repent o' your words," said Gallagher, and his brow darkened as he spoke.

"Time was," said the old man, "when I had something surer than grey hairs to make such as you respect me;" and he drew himself up with an air of patriarchal dignity, and displayed in his still expansive chest and commanding height, the remains of a noble figure, that bore testimony to the truth of what he had just uttered. The old man's eye kindled as he spoke—but 'twas only for a moment; and the expression of pride and defiance was succeeded by that of coldness and contempt.

"I'd have beat you blind the best day ever you seen," said Gallagher, with an impudent swagger.

"Troth you wouldn't, Gallagher," said a contemporary of the old man: "but your consait bates the world!"

"That's true," said Rooney. "He's a great man intirely, in his own opinion. I'd make a power of money if I could *buy* Gallagher at *my* price, and *sell* him at his *own*."

A low and jeering laugh followed this hit of my friend Rooney; and Gallagher assumed an aspect so lowering, that a peasant, standing near me, turned to his companion and said, significantly, "By gor, Ned there'll be wigs on the green afore long!"

And he was quite right.

The far off speck on the horizon, whence the prophetic eye of a sailor can foretel the coming storm, is not more nicely discriminated by the mariner, than the symptoms of an approaching fray by an Irishman; and scarcely had the foregoing words been uttered, than I saw the men tucking up their long frieze coats in a sort of jacket fashion— thus getting rid of their *tails,* like game-cocks before a battle. A more menacing grip was taken by the bearer of each stick (a usual appendage of Hibernians); and a general closing-in of the bystanders round the nucleus of dissatisfaction, made it perfectly apparent that hostilities must soon commence.

I was not long left in suspense about such a catastrophe, for a general outbreak soon took place, commencing in the centre with the principals already noticed, and radiating throughout the whole circle, until a general action ensued, and the belligerents were dispersed in various hostile groups over the churchyard.

I was a spectator from the topmost step of a stile leading into the burial-ground, deeming it imprudent to linger within the precincts of the scene of action, when my attention was attracted by the appearance of a horseman, who galloped up the little stony road, and was no sooner at my side, than he dismounted, exclaiming, at the top of his voice, "Oh! you reprobates, *lave* off, I tell you, you heathens! Are you Christians at all?"

I must here pause a moment to describe the person of the horseman in question. He was a tall, thin, pale man—having a hat, which from exposure to bad weather, had its broad slouching brim crimped into many fantastic involutions—its crown somewhat depressed in the middle, and the edges of the same exhibiting a napless paleness; very far removed from its original black; no shirt-collar sheltered his angular jaw bones—a narrow white cravat was drawn tightly round his spare neck—a single-breasted coat of rusty black, with standing collar, was tightly buttoned nearly up to his chin, and a nether garment of the same, with large silver knee-buckles, meeting a square-cut and buckram-like pair of black leather boots, with heavy, plated spurs, that had seen the best of their days, completed the picture. His horse was a small well-built hack, whose long rough coat would have been white, but that soiled litter had stained it to a dirty yellow; and taking advantage of the liberty which the abandoned rein afforded, he very quietly turned him to the little fringe of grass which bordered each side of the path, to make as much profit of his time as he might, before his rider should resume his seat in the old high-pommelled saddle which he had vacated, in uttering the ejaculation I have recorded.

This person then, hastily mounting the stile on which I stood, with rustic politeness said, "By your leave, Sir," as he pushed by me in haste, and jumping from the top of the wall, proceeded with long and rapid strides towards the combatants, and brandishing a heavy thong whip which he carried, he began to lay about him with equal vigour and impartiality on each and every of the peace-breakers, both parties sharing in the castigation thus bestowed, with the most even, and, I might add, *heavy*-handed justice.

My surprise was great on finding that all the blows inflicted by this new belligerent, instead of being resented by the assaulted parties, seemed taken as if resistance against this potent chastiser were vain, and in a short time they all fled before him, like so many frightened school-boys before an incensed peda-gogue, and huddled themselves together in a crowd, which at once became pacified at his presence.

Seeing this result, I descended from my perch, and ran towards the scene that excited my surprise in no ordinary degree. I found this new-comer delivering to the multitude he had quelled, a severe reproof of their "unchristian doings," as he termed them; and it became evident that he was the pastor of the flock, and it must be acknowledged, a very turbulent flock, he seemed to have of it.

This admonition was soon ended. It was certainly impressive, and well calculated for the audience to whom it was delivered, as well as from the simplicity of its language as the solemnity of its manner, which was much enhanced by the deep and somewhat sepulchral voice of the speaker. "And now," added the pastor, "let me ask you for what you were fight-ing like so many wild Indians; for surely your con-duct is liker to savage creatures than men that have been bred up in the hearing of God's word?"

A pause of a few seconds followed this question; and, at length, some one ventured to answer from amongst the crowd, that it was "in regard of the berrin."

"And is not so solemn a sight," asked the priest, "as the burial of the departed, enough to keep down the evil passions of your hearts?"

"Troth then, and plaze your Riverince, it was nothin' ill-nathured in life, but only a good-nathured turn we wor doin' for poor Paudeen Mooney that's departed; and sure it's to your Riverince we'll be goin' immadiantly for the masses for the poor boy's sowl." Thus making interest in the offended quarter, with an address for which the Irish peasant is pre-eminently distinguished.

"Tut! tut!" rapidly answered the priest; anxious, perhaps, to silence this very palpable appeal to his own interest. "Don't talk to me about doing a good-natured turn. Not," added he, in a subdued under-tone, "but that prayers for the souls of the faithful departed are enjoined by the church; but what has that to do with your scandalous and lawless doings that I witnessed this minute? and you yourself," said he, addressing the last speaker, "one of the busiest with your alpeen? I'm afraid you're rather fractious, Rooney—take care that I don't speak to you from the altar."

"Oh, God forbid that your Riverince id have to do the like," said the mother of the deceased, already noticed, in an imploring tone, and with the big teardrops chasing each other down her cheeks; "and sure it was only they wanted to put my poor boy in the ground *first,* and no wondher sure, as your Riverince *knows,* and not to have my poor Paudeen——"

"Tut! tut! woman," interrupted the priest, waving his hand rather impatiently, "don't let me hear any folly."

"I ax your Riverince's pardon, and sure it's myself that id be sorry to offind my clargy—God's blessin' be an them night and day! But I was only goin' to put in a word for Mikee Rooney, and sure it wasn't him at all, nor wauldn't be any of us, only for Shan Gallagher, that wouldn't lave us in peace."

"Gallagher!" said the priest in a deeply-reproachful tone. "Where is he?"

Gallagher came not forward, but the crowd drew back, and left him revealed to the priest. His aspect was that of sullen indifference, and he seemed to be the only person present totally uninfluenced by the presence of his pastor, who now advanced towards him, and extending his attenuated hand in the attitude of denunciation towards the offender, said very solemnly—

"I have already spoken to you in the house of worship, and now, once more, I warn you to beware. Riot and battle are found wherever you go, and if you do not speedily reform your course of life, I shall expel you from the pale of the church, and pronounce sentence of excommunication upon you from the altar."

Every one appeared awed by the solemnity and severity of this address from the onset, but when the word "excommunication" was uttered, a thrill of horror seemed to run through the assembled multitude: and even Gallagher himself I thought betrayed some emotion on hearing the terrible word. Yet he evinced it but for a moment, and turning on his heel, he retired from the ground with something of the swagger with which he entered it. The crowd opened to let him pass, and opened widely, as if they sought to avoid contact with one so fearfully denounced.

"You have two coffins here," said the clergyman, "proceed, therefore, immediately to make two graves, and let the bodies be interred at the same time, and I will read the service for the dead."

No very great time was consumed in making the necessary preparation. The "narrow beds" were made, and, as their tenants were consigned to their last long sleep, the solemn voice of the priest was raised in the "De Profundis;" and when he had concluded the short and beautiful psalm, the friends of the deceased closed the graves, and covered them neatly with fresh-cut sods, which is what *Paddy* very metaphorically calls

Putting the daisy quilt over him.

The clergyman retired from the church-yard, and I followed his footsteps for the purpose of introducing myself to "his reverence," and seeking from him an explanation of what was still a most unfathomable mystery to me, namely the cause of the quarrel, which, from certain passages in his address to the people, I saw he understood, though so slightly glanced at. Accordingly, I overtook the priest, and as the Irish song has it,

To him I obnoxiously made my approaches.

He received me with courtesy, which though not savouring much of intercourse with polished circles, seemed to spring whence all true politeness emanates—from a good heart.

I begged to assure him it was not an impertinent curiosity that made me desirous of becoming acquainted with the cause of the fray which I had witnessed, and he had put a stop to in so summary a manner, and hoped he would not consider it an intrusion if I applied to him for that purpose.

"No intrusion in life, Sir," answered the priest very frankly, and with a rich *brogue,* whose intonation was singularly expressive of good nature. It was the specimen of brogue I have never met but in one class, the Irish gentleman of the last century—an accent, which, though it possessed all the characteristic traits of "the brogue," was at the time divested of the slightest trace of vulgarity. This is not to be met with now, or at least very rarely. An attempt has been made by those who fancy it genteel, to graft the English accent upon the Broguish stem—and a very bad fruit it has produced. The truth is, the accents of the two countries could never be happily blended; and far from making a pleasing amalgamation, it conveys the idea that the speaker is endeavouring to *escape* from his own accent for what he considers a superior one; and it is this attempt to be fine, which so particularly allies the idea of vulgarity with the tone of brogue so often heard in the present day.

Such, I have said, was *not* the brogue of the Rev. Phelim Roach, or Father Roach, as the peasants called him; and his voice, which I have earlier noticed as almost sepulchral, I found derived that character from the feeling of the speaker when engaged in an admonitory address; for when employed on colloquial occasions, it was no more than what might be called a rich and deep manly voice. So much for Father Roach, who forthwith proceeded to enlighten me on the subject of the funeral, and the quarrel arising therefrom.

"The truth is, Sir, these poor people are possessed of many foolish superstitions; and however we may, as *men,* pardon them, looking upon them as fictions originating in a warm imagination, and finding a ready admission into the minds of an unlettered and susceptible peasantry, we cannot, as pastors of the flock, admit their belief to the poor people committed to our care."

This was quite new to me; to find a clergyman of the religion I had hitherto heard of as being *par excellence* abounding in superstition, denouncing the very article in question.—But let me not interrupt Father Roach.

"The superstition I speak of," continued he, "is one of the many these warm-hearted people indulge in, and is certainly very poetical in its texture.

"But, Sir," interrupted my newly-made acquaintance, pulling forth a richly chased gold watch of antique workmanship, that at once suggested ideas of the *'bon vieux temps,'* "I must ask your pardon—I have an engagement to keep at the little hut I call my home, which obliges me to proceed there forthwith. If you have so much time to spare as will enable you to walk with me to the end of this little road, it will suffice to make you acquainted with the nature of the superstition in question."

I gladly assented; and the priest, disturbing the nibbling occupation of his hack, threw the rein over his arm, and the docile little beast following him on one side as quietly as I did on the other, he gave me the following account of the cause of all the previous riot, as we wound down the little stony path that led to the main road.

"There is a belief among the peasantry in this particular district, that the ghost of the last person interred in the church-yard, is obliged to traverse, unceasingly, the road between this earth and purgatory, carrying water to slake the burning thirst of

those confined in that 'limbo large;' and that the
ghost is thus obliged to walk

> Through the dead waste and middle of the night,

until some fresh arrival of a tenant to the 'narrow
house,' supplies a fresh ghost to 'relieve guard,' if I
may be allowed so military an expression; and thus,
the supply of water to the sufferers in purgatory is
kept up unceasingly."

Hence it was that the fray had arisen, and the poor
mother's invocation, "that her darling boy should
not be left to wander about the church-yard dark
and lone in the long nights," became at once intelli-
gible. Father Roach gave me some curious illustra-
tions of the different ways in which this superstition
influenced his "poor people," as he constantly called
them; but I suppose my readers have had quite
enough of the subject, and I shall therefore say no
more of other "cases in point," contented with having given them one example, and recording the existence of a superstition, which, however wild,
undoubtedly owes its existence to an affectionate
heart and a poetic imagination.

The Red Pony

の

[TRANSCRIBED BY WILLIAM LARMINIE]

Narrator, P. Minahan,
Malinmore County, Donegal

There was a poor man there. He had a great family of sons. He had no means to put them forward. He had them at school. One day, when they were coming from school, he thought that whichever of them was last at the door he would keep him out. It was the youngest of the family was last at the door. The father shut the door. He would not let him in. The boy went weeping. He would not let him in till night came. The father said he would never let him in; that he had boys enough.

The lad went away. He was walking till night. He came to a house on the rugged side of a hill on a height, one feather giving it shelter and support. He went in. He got a place till morning. When he made his breakfast in the morning, he was going. The man of the house made him a present of a red pony, a saddle, and bridle. He went riding on the pony. He went away with himself.

"Now," said the pony, "whatever thing you may see before you, don't touch it."

They went on with themselves. He saw a light before him on the high-road. When he came as far as the light, there was an open box on the road, and a light coming up out of it. He took up the box. There was a lock of hair in it.

"Are you going to take up the box?" said the pony.

"I am. I cannot go past it."

"It's better for you to leave it," said the pony.

He took up the box. He put it in his pocket. He was going with himself. A gentleman met him.

"Pretty is your little beast. Where are you going?"

"I am looking for service."

"I am in want of one like you, among the stable boys."

He hired the lad. The lad said he must get room for the little beast in the stable. The gentleman said he would get it. They went home then. He had eleven boys. When they were going out into the stable at ten o'clock each of them took a light but he. He took no candle at all with him.

Each of them went to his own stable. When he went into his stable he opened the box. He left it in a hole in the wall. The light was great. It was twice

as much as in the other stables. There was wonder
on the boys what was the reason of the light being
so great, and he without a candle with him at all.
They told the master they did not know what was
the cause of the light with the last boy. They had
given him no candle, and he had twice as much light
as they had.

"Watch to-morrow night what kind of light he
has," said the master.

They watched the night of the morrow. They saw
the box in the hole that was in the wall, and the light
coming out of the box. They told the master. When
the boys came to the house, the king asked him what
was the reason why he did not take a candle to the
stable, as well as the other boys. The lad said he had a
candle. The king said he had not. He asked him how
he got the box from which the light came. He said
he had no box. The king said he had, and that he
must give it to him; that he would not keep him
unless he gave him the box. The boy gave it to him.
The king opened it. He drew out the lock of hair, in
which was the light.

"You must go," said the king, "and bring me the
woman, to whom the hair belongs."

The lad was troubled. He went out. He told the
red pony.

"I told you not to take up the box. You will get
more than that on account of the box. When you

have made your breakfast to-morrow, put the saddle and bridle on me."

When he made his breakfast on the morning of the morrow, he put saddle and bridle on the pony. He went till they came to three miles of sea.

"Keep a good hold now. I am going to give a jump over the sea. When I arrive yonder there is a fair on the strand. Every one will be coming up to you to ask for a ride, because I am such a pretty little beast. Give no one a ride. You will see a beautiful woman drawing near you, her in whose hair was the wonderful light. She will come up to you. She will ask you to let her ride for a while. Say you will and welcome. When she comes riding, I will be off."

When she came to the sea, she cleared the three miles at a jump. She came upon the land opposite, and every one was asking for a ride upon the beast, she was that pretty. He was giving a ride to no one. He saw that woman in the midst of the people. She was drawing near. She asked him would he give her a little riding. He said he would give it, and a hundred welcomes. She went riding. She went quietly till she got out of the crowd. When the pony came to the sea she made the three-mile jump again, the beautiful woman along with her. She took her home to the king. There was great joy on the king to see her. He took her into the parlour. She said to him, she would not marry any one until he would get the

bottle of healing water that was in the eastern world.
The king said to the lad he must go and bring the
bottle of healing water that was in the eastern world
to the lady. The lad was troubled. He went to the
pony. He told the pony he must go to the eastern
world for the bottle of healing water that was in it,
and bring it to the lady.

"My advice was good," said the pony, "on the day
you took the box up. Put saddle and bridle on me."

He went riding on her. They were going till they
came to the sea. She stood then.

"You must kill me," said the pony; "that, or I must
kill you."

"It is hard to me to kill you," said the boy. "If I
kill you there will be no way to myself."

He cut her belly down. He opened it up. She was
not long opened when there came two black ravens
and one small one. The two ravens went into the
body. They drank their fill of the blood. When they
came out the little raven went in. He closed the
belly of the pony. He would not let the little bird
come out till he got the bottle of healing water was
in the eastern world. The ravens were very troubled. They were begging him to let the little bird
out. He said he would not let it out till they brought
him the bottle. They went to seek the bottle. They
came back and there was not bottle with them.
They were entreating him to let the bird out to

them. He would not let the bird out till he got the bottle. They went away again for the bottle. They came at evening. They were tossed and scorched, and they had the bottle. They came to the place where the pony was. They gave the bottle to the boy. He rubbed the healing water to every place where they were burned. Then he let out the little bird. There was great joy on them to see him. He rubbed some of the healing water to the place where he cut the pony. He spilt a drop into her ear. She arose as well as she ever was. He had a little bottle in his pocket. He put some of the healing water into it. They went home.

When the king perceived the pony coming he rose out. He took hold of her with his two hands. He took her in. He smothered her with kisses and drowned her with tears: he dried her with finest cloths of silk and satin.

This is what the lady was doing while they were away. She boiled pitch and filled a barrel, and that boiling. Now she went beside it and stripped herself. She rubbed the healing water to herself. She came out; she went to the barrel, naked. She gave a jump in and out of the barrel. Three times she went in and out. She said she would never marry any one who could not do the same. The young king came. He stripped himself. He went to the barrel. He fell half in, half out.

He was all boiled and burned. Another gentleman came. He stripped himself. He gave a jump into the barrel. He was burned. He came not out till he died. After that there was no one going in or out. The barrel was there, and no one at all was going near it. The lad went up to it and stripped himself. He rubbed the healing water on himself. He came to the barrel. He jumped in and out three times. He was watching her. She came out. She said she would never marry any one but him.

Came the priest of the pattens, and the clerk of the bells. The pair were married. The wedding lasted three nights and three days. When it was over, the lad went to look at the place where the pony was. He never remembered to go and see the pony during the wedding. He found nothing but a heap of bones. There were two champions and two young girls playing cards. The lad went crying when he saw the bones of the pony. One of the girls asked what was the matter with him. He said it was all one to her; that she cared nothing for his troubles.

"I would like to get knowledge of the cause why you are crying."

"It is my pony who was here. I never remembered to see her during the wedding. I have nothing now but her bones. I don't know what I shall do after her. It was she who did all that I accomplished."

The girl went laughing. "Would you know your pony if you saw her?"

"I would know," said he.

She laid aside the cards. She stood up.

"Isn't that your pony?" said she.

"It is," he said.

"I was the pony," said the girl, "and the two ravens who went in to drink my blood my two brothers. When the ravens came out, a little bird went in. You closed the pony. You would not let the little bird out till they brought the bottle of healing water that was in the eastern world. They brought the bottle to you. The little bird was my sister. It was my brothers were the ravens. We were all under enchantments. It is my sister who is married to you. The enchantments are gone from us since she was married."

A Little Captive Maid

[SARAH ORNE JEWETT]

I

The early winter twilight was falling over the town of Kenmare, a heavy open carriage with some belated travellers bounced and rattled along the smooth highway, hurrying toward the inn and a night's lodging. Two slender young figures drew back together into the leafless hedge by the roadside and stood there, whispering and keeping fast hold of hands after the simple fashion of children and lovers. There was an empty bird's nest close beside them, and they looked at that, and after they had watched the carriage a moment, and even laughed because Dinny Killoren, the driver, had recognized their presence by a loud snap of his whip, they still loitered. The girl turned away from her lover, who only looked at her, and felt the soft lining of the nest with the fingers of her left hand. Johnny Morris's handsome young face looked pinched and sad in the gray dampness of the dusk.

"The poor tidy cr'atures!" said Nora Connelly. "Look now at their little house, Johnny, how nate it is, and they gone from it. I mind the birds singing in the hedge one day last summer, and I walking by in the road."

"Wisha, 'tis our own tidy house I'm thinking of," said Johnny, reproachfully; "I've long dr'amed of it, and now whatever will I do and you gone away to Ameriky? Faix, it's too hard for us, Norry dear; we'll get no luck from your goin'; 'twas the Lord mint us for 'ach other!"

"I'm safe to come back, darling," said Nora, troubled by her lover's lamentations. "'Tis for the love of you I'm going, sure, Johnny dear! I suppose 'tis yourself won't want me then aither when I come back; sure they says folks dries all up there and gets brown and small with the heat that's in it. Promise now that you'll say nothing, so long as I'm fine an' rich coming home!"

"Don't break me heart, Nora, with your wild talk; who else but yourself would be joking, and our hearts breaking with the parting, and this our last walk together," mourned the young man. "Come, darling, we must be going on. 'Tis a good way yet through the town, an' your aunt ready to have my life now for not sinding you back at t'ree o'clock."

"Let her wait!" said Nora, scornfully. "I'll be free of her, then, this time to-morrow. 'Tis herself 'll be keenin' after me as if 'twas wakin' me she was, and the heart of stone that's inside her and no tears to her eyes. They might be glass buttons in her old head, they might then! I'd love you to the last day I lived, John Morris, if 'twas only to have the joke on her," and Nora's eyes sparkled with fun. "I'd spite her if I could, the old crow! Sorra a bit of l'ave takin' have I got from her yet, but to say I must sind home my passage-money inside the first month I'm out. Oh, but, Johnny, I'll be so lonesome there; 'tis a cold home I had since me mother died, but God help me when I'm far from it. The girl and her lover were both crying now; Johnny kissed her and put his arm tenderly about her, there where they stood alone by the roadside; both knew that the dreaded hour of parting had come.

Presently, as if moved by the stern hand of fate rather than by their own will, they walked away along the road, still weeping. They came into the town, where lights were bright in the houses. There was the usual cheerful racket about the inn. The Lansdowne Arms seemed to be unusually populous and merry for a winter night. Somebody called to Johnny Morris from a doorway, but he did not answer. Close by were the ruins of the old abbey, and he drew Nora with him between the two stones which made a narrow entrance way to the grounds. It was dreary enough there among the wintry shadows, the solemn shapes of the crumbling ruin, and the rustling trees.

"Tell me now once more that you love me, darlin'," sobbed the poor lad; "you're goin' away from me, Nora, an' 'tis you'll find it aisy to forget. Everything you l'ave will be spakin' to me of you. Oh, Nora, Nora! howiver will I l'ave you go to Ameriky; I was no man at all, or why didn't I forbid it? 'Tis only I was too poor to keep you back, God help me!"

"Be quiet now," said Nora. "I'll not forget you. I'll save all my money till I'll come back to you. We're young, dear lad, sure; kiss me now an' say good-by, my fine gay lad, and then walk home quiet wid me through the town. I call the holy saints to hear me that I won't forget."

And so they kissed and parted, and walked home quiet through the town as Nora had desired. She stopped here and there for a parting word with a friend, and there was even a sense of dignity and consequence in the poor child's simple heart because she was going to set forth on her great journey the next morning, while others would ignobly remain in Kenmare. Thank God, she had no father and mother to undergo the pain of seeing her disappear forever from their eyes. The poor heart-broken Irish folk who let their young sons and daughters go away from them to America, who of us has stopped half long enough to think of their sorrows and to pity them? What must it be to see the little companies set forth on their way to the sea, knowing that they will return no more? The fever for emigration is a heart-rending sort of epidemic, and the boys and girls who dream of riches and pleasure until they are impatient of their homes in poor, beautiful Ireland! alas, they sail away on the crowded ships to find hard work and hard fare, and know their mistakes about finding a fairy land too late, too late! And Nora Connelly's aunt had hated Johnny Morris, and laid this scheme for separating them, under cover of the furtherance of Nora's wellfare. They had been lovers from their childhood, and Johnny's mother, from whom Nora had just parted on that last sad evening, was a sickly woman and poor as poverty. Johnny was like son and daughter both, he could never leave her while she lived; they had needed all of Nora's cheerfulness and love, and now they were going to lose her, perhaps forever. Everybody knew how few came back from America, no wonder that these Irish hearts were sad with parting.

On the morrow there was little time for leave-takings. Some people tried to make it a day of jokes and festivities when such parties of emigrants left the country-side, but there was always too much sadness underneath the laughter; and the chilly rain fell that day as if Ireland herself wept for her wandering children—poor Ireland, who gives the best of them to the great busy countries over seas, and longs for the time when she can be rich and busy herself, and keep the young people at home and happy in field and town. What does the money cost that comes back to the cottage households broken as if by death? What does it cost to the aching hearts of fathers and mothers, to the homesick lads and girls in America, with the cold Atlantic between them and home?

II

The winter day was clear and cold, with a hint of coming spring in the blue sky. As you came up Barry Street, the main thoroughfare of a thriving American town, you could not help noticing the thick elm-branches overhead and the long rows of country horses and sleighs before the stores, and a general look of comfortably-mingled country and city life.

The high-storied offices and warehouses came to an end just where the hill began to rise, and on the slope, to the left, was a terraced garden planted thick with fruit-trees and flowering shrubbery. Above this stood a large old-fashioned white house close to the street. At first sight one was pleased with its look of comfort and provincial elegance, but, as you approached, the whole lower story seemed unused. If you glanced up at a window of the second story you were likely to see an elderly gentleman looking out, pale and unhappy, as if invalidism and its enforced idleness were peculiarly hard for him to bear. Sometimes you might catch sight of the edge of a newspaper, but there was never a book in his hand, there was never a child's face looking out to companion the old man. People always spoke of poor old Captain Balfour nowadays, but only a few months before he had been the leading business man of the city, absorbed in a dozen different enterprises. A widower and childless, he felt himself to be alone indeed in this time of illness and despondency. Early in life he had followed the sea, from choice, not necessity, but for many years he had been master of the old house and garden on Barry Street, his inherited home. People always spoke of him with deference and respect, they pitied him now in his rich and pitiful old age. In the early autumn a stroke of paralysis had dulled and disabled him, and its effect was more and more puzzling and irritating beside to the captain's pride.

He more and more insisted upon charging his long captivity and uncomfortable condition at the doors of his medical advisers and the household. At first, in dark and gloomy weather, or in days of unusual depression, a running fire of comments was kept up toward those who treated him like a child, and who made an apothecary's shop of his stomach, and kept him upon such incomprehensible diet. A slice of salt beef and a captain's biscuit were indignantly demanded at these times, but it was touching to observe that the person in actual attendance was always treated with extreme consideration or even humble gratitude, while the offenders were always absent. *"They* were guilty of all the wrongs and kept the captain miserable; *they* were impersonal foes of his peace; there never was anything but a kind word for Mrs. Nash, the housekeeper, or Reilly, the faithful attendant; there never were any personal rebukes administered to the cook; and as for the doctor, Captain Balfour treated him as one gentleman should treat another.

Until early in January, when once in a while even the hitherto respected Mrs. Nash was directly accused of a total lack of judgment, and James Reilly could not do or say anything to suit, and the lives of these honest persons became nearly unbearable; the maid under Mrs. Nash's charge (for the household had always been kept up exactly as in Mrs. Balfour's day) could not be expected to consider the captain's condition and her own responsibilities as his older and deeply attached companions could, and, tired of the dulness and idleness of the old house, fell to that state where dismissal was inevitable. Then neither Mrs. Nash nor Reilly knew what to do next, they were not as young as they had been, and to use their own words, minded the stairs. At last Reilly, a sensible Irishman, proposed a change in the order of house-keeping. The captain might never come downstairs any more, they could shut up the dining-room and the parlors, and make their daily work much lighter.

"An' I won't say that I haven't got word for you of a tidy little girl," said Reilly, beseechingly. "She's a relation to my cousins the Donahues and as busy as a sparrow. She'll work beside you an' the cook like your own shild, she will that, Mrs. Nash, and is a light-hearted shild the day through. She's just over too, the little greenhorn!"

"Perhaps she'll be just what we want, Reilly," agreed the housekeeper, after reflection. "Send her up to see me this very evening, if you're going where she is."

So the very next day into the desolate old house came young Nora Connelly, a true child of the old country, with a laughing gray eye and a smooth girlish cheek, and a pretty touch of gold at the edge of the fair brown hair about her forehead. It was a serious

little face, not beautiful, except in its delightful girlish-
ness. She was a friendly, kindly little creature, fond of
her simple pleasures and willing to work hard the day
through. The great house itself was a treasure-house
of new experience, and she felt her position in the
captain's family to be a valued promotion.

One morning, life looked very dark to the master.
Everything had been going wrong since breakfast,
and the captain rang for Reilly when he had just
gone out, and Mrs. Nash was busy with a messenger.

"Go up, will you, Nora?" she said, anxiously, "and
say that I'll be there in a minute. Reilly's just left
him——"

And Nora sped away, nothing loath; she had never
taken a satisfactory look at the master, and this was
the fourth day since she had come to the house.

She opened the door and saw a handsome, fretful,
tired old gentleman, whose newspaper had slipped
from his hand and gone out of reach. She hurried to
pick it up without being told.

"Who are you?" inquired the captain, looking at
her with considerable interest.

"Nora Connelly, sir," said the girl in a delicious
Irish voice. "I'm your new maid, sir, since Winsday. I
feel very sorry for your bein' sick, sir."

"There's nothing the matter with me," growled the captain, unexpectedly.

"Wisha, sir, I'm glad of that!" said Nora, with a wag of her head like a bird, and a light in her eye. "Mrs. Nash'll be here at once, sir, for your ordhers. She is d'aling wid a boy below in the hall. You are looking fine an' comfortable the day, sir."

"I never was so uncomfortable in my life," said the captain. "You can open that window."

"And it snowing fast, sir? You'll let out all the fine heat; heat's very dear now and cold is cheap, so it is, with poor folks. 'Tis a great pity you've no turfs now to keep your fire in for you. 'Tis very strange there do be no turf in this foine country," and she looked at the captain with a winning smile. The captain smiled back again in spite of himself.

Nora stood looking out of the window; she seemed to be thinking of herself instead of the invalid.

"What did you say your name was?" asked the old gentleman, a moment later, frowning his eyebrows at her like pieces of artillery.

"Please, sir, I'm Nora Connelly, from the outside o' Kenmare." She made him the least bit of a curtsey, as if a sudden wind had bent her like a long-stemmed flower.

"How came you here?" His mouth straightened into a smile as he spoke, in spite of a determination to be severe.

"I'm but two weeks over, sir. I come over to me cousins, the Donahues, seeking me fortune. I'd like Ameriky, 'tis a fine place, sir, but I'm very homesick intirely. I'm as fast to be going back as I was to be coming away," and she gave a soft sigh and turned away to brush the hearth.

"Well, you must be a good girl," said the captain, with great propriety, after a pause.

"'Deed, sir, I am that," responded Nora, sincerely. "No one had a word to fling afther me and I coming away, but crying afther me. Nobody'll tell anything to my shame when my name'll be spoke at home. My mother brought me up well, God save her, she did, then!"

This unaffected report of her own good reputation was pleasing to Nora's employer; the sight of Nora's simple, pleasant Irish face and the freshness of her youth was the most delightful thing that had happened in many a dreary day. He felt in his waistcoat pocket with sudden impulse, sure of finding a bit of money there with which Nora Connelly might buy herself a ribbon. He was strongly inclined toward making her feel at home in the old house which had grown to be such a prison to himself. But there was no money in the pocket, as there always used to be when he was well. He had not needed any before in a long time. He began to fret about this and to wonder what they had done with his pocket-book; it was ignominious to be treated like a schoolboy. While he brooded over his wrongs, Nora heard Mrs. Nash's hurrying footsteps in the hall, but as she slipped away it was plain that she had found time enough to bestow her entire sympathy, and even affection, upon the captain in this brief interview.

"He's dull, poor gentleman—he's very sad all day by himself, and so pleasant spoken, the crathur!" she said to herself, indignantly, as she went running down the stairs.

It was not long before, to everybody's surprise, Captain Balfour gained strength, and began to feel so much better, that Nora was often posted in the room or the hall close by to run his frequent errands and pick up his newspapers as they fell. This gave Mrs. Nash and Reilly a chance to look after their other business affairs, and to take their ease after so long a season of close attendance. The captain had a gruff way of asking, "Where's that little girl?" as if he only wished to see her to scold her roundly; and Nora was always ready to come with her sewing or any bit of housework that could be carried and to entertain her master by the hour. The more irritable his temper, the more unconscious and merry she always seemed.

"I was down last night wid me cousins, so I was," she informed him one morning, while she brushed up the floor about the fireplace on her hands and knees. "You'd ought to see her little shild, sir, indade she's the darling cr'ature. I never saw anyone so crabbed and smart for the size of her. She ain't the heighth of a bee's knee, sir!"

"Who isn't?" inquired the captain, absently, attracted for the moment by the pleasing simile.

"Me cousin's little shild, sir," answered Nora, appealingly, with a fear that she had failed in her choice of a subject. "'Tis no more than the heighth of a bee's knee she is, the colleen, and has every talk to you like a little grandmother—the big words of her haves to come sideways out of her mouth. I'd like it well if her mother would dress her up prertty, and I'd go fetch her for you to see."

The captain made an expressive sound of disdain, and Nora brushed away at the rug in silence. He looked out of the window and drummed on the arm of his chair. It was a very uncomfortable morning. There was a noise in the street, and Nora pricked up her ears with her head alert like a young hare, stood up on her knees, and listened.

"I'll warrant it's me heart's darlin' tooting at the fife," she exclaimed.

"Nothing but a parcel of boys," grumbled the captain.

"Faix it's he, thin, the dacint lad!" said Nora, by this time close to the other front window. "Look at him now, sir, goin' by! He's alther b'y in the church and a lovely voice in him. Me cousins is going to have him learn music. That's 'The girl I left behind me,' he's got in the old fife now."

"Hard to tell what it is," growled the captain. "Anything for a racket, I dare say."

"Faix, sir, I was thinking meself the tune come out of him tail first," agreed Nora, with ready sympathy "He's the big brother to the little sisther I told you of just now. 'Twas Dan Sullivan gave Johnny the old fife; himself used to play it in a company. There's a kay or two gone, I'm misthrusting, anyway there's teeth gone in the tune."

Nora was again brushing the floor industriously. The captain was listless and miserable: the silence vexed him even more than the harmless prattle.

"I used to play the flute pretty well myself when I was a young man," he said pleasantly, after a while.

"I'd like well to hear you, then," said Nora, enthusiastically. She was only making an excuse of the brushing to linger with him a little while. "Oh, but your honor would have liked to hear me mother sing. God give her rest, but she had the lovely voice for you! They'd be sinding for her from three towns away to sing with the fiddle for weddings and dances. If you'd hear her sing the 'Pride of Glencoe' 'twould take the heart out of you, it would indade."

"My wife was a most beautiful singer when she was young. I like to hear a pretty voice," said the captain sadly.

"'Twas me dear mother had it, then," answered Nora. "I do be often minding her singing when I'm falling asleep. I hear her voice very plain sometimes. My mother was from the North, sir, and she had tunes that didn't be known to the folks about Kenmare. 'Inniskillen Dragoon' was one of the best liked, and it went lovely with the wheel when she'd be spinning. Everybody'd be calling for her to sing that tune. Strangers would come and ask her for a song that were passing through the town. There was great talk always of me mother's singing, they'd know of her for twinty miles round. Whin I see the fire gone down in red coals like this, all red like our turf at home, and it do be growing dark, I remimber well 'twas such times she'd sing like a bird for us, being through her long day's work, an' all of us round the fire kaping warm if we could a winter night. Oh, but she'd sing then like a lark in the fields, God rest her!"

Nora brushed away a tear and blessed herself. "You'd like well to hear me mother sing, sir, I'm telling you God's truth," she said, simply. And the old captain watched her and smiled as if he were willing to hear more.

"Folks would pay her well, too. They'd all be afraid she'd stop when she'd once begin. There was nobody but herself could sing with the fiddle. I mind she came home one morning when she'd been sint for to a great wedding—'twas a man's only daughter that owned his own land. And me mother came home to us wid a collection of twilve and eight-pince tied up in her best apron corner. We'd as good as a wedding ourselves out of it too; 'twas she had the spinding hand, the crathur; and we had a roast goose that same night and asked fri'nds to it. Folks don't have the good fun here they has in the old country, sir, so they don't."

"There used to be good times here," said the poor old captain.

"I'm thinking 'twould be dale the better if you wint and stayed for a while over there," urged the girl, affectionately. "It'll soon be comin' green and illigant while its winther here still; the gorse'll be blooming, sir, and the little daisies thick under your two feet, and you'd be sitting out in the warm rain and sun and feeling the good of the ground. If you'd go to Glengariff I think you'd be soon well, I do, then, Captain Balfour, your honor, sir."

"I'm too old, Nora," replied the captain, dismally, but not without interest.

"Sure there ain't a boy in the town that has the spark in his eye like yourself, sir," responded Nora, with encouraging heartiness. "I'd break away from these sober old folks and the docthers and all, and take ship, and you'd be soon over the say, and live like a lord in the first cabin, and you'd land aisy on the tinder in the cove o' Cork and slape that night in the city, and go next day to the Eccles Hotel in Glengariff. Oh, wisha, the fine place it is wid the say forninst the garden wall. You'd get a swim in the clane salt wather, and be as light as a bird. Sure I wouldn't be t'ased wid so much docthoring and advising, and you none the betther wid it."

"Why couldn't I have a swim in the sea here?" inquired the captain, indulgently.

"Sure, it wouldn't be the same at all," responded Nora, with contempt. "'Tis the say-shore of the old country will do you the most good. The say is very salt entirely by Glengariff, the bay runs up to it, and you'd get a strong boatman would row you up and down, and you'd walk in the green lanes and the folks in the houses would give you good day; and whin you'd be afther givin' old Mother Casey a trippence, she'd down on her two little knees and pray for your honor till you'd be running home like a light horseman."

The old man laughed heartily for the first time that day. "I used to be the fastest runner of any lad in school," he said, with pride.

"Sure you might thry it again, wid Mrs. Casey's kind help, sir," insisted the girl. "Now go to Glengariff this next month o' May, sir, do!"

"Perhaps I will," said the captain, decidedly. "I'm not going to keep up this sort of thing much longer, I can tell them that! If they can't do me any good they may say so, and I'll steer my own course. That's a good idea about the salt water."

The old man fell into a pleasant sleep, with a contented smile on his face. The fire flickered and snapped, and Nora sat still looking into it; her thoughts were far away. Perhaps her unkind aunt would find means to stop the letters between Johnny Morris and herself. Oh, if her mother were only alive, if the scattered household were once more together! It would be a long time at this rate, before she could go back to Johnny with a hundred pounds.

The fire settled itself together and sent up a bright blaze. The old man opened his eyes and looked bewildered; she stepped quickly to his side. "You'll be askin' for Mr. Reilly?" she said.

"No, no," responded the captain, firmly. "What was the name of that place you were talking about?"

"Whiddy Island, sir, where me father was born?" Nora's thoughts had wandered far and wide, she was thinking that she had heard that land was cheap on Whiddy and the fishing fine. She and Johnny had often thought they might do better than in Kenmare.

"No, no," said the captain again, sternly.

"Oh, Glengariff," she exclaimed. "Yes, sir, we were talking—"

"That's it," responded the captain, complacently. "I should like to know something more about the place."

"I was never in it but twice," exclaimed Nora, "but 'twas lovely there intirely. My father had a time of fishin', and 'twas one summer we left Kenmare and went to a place, Baltimore was the name, beyond Glengariff itself, toward the illigant town of Bantry, sir. I saw Bantry, sir, when I was young. We were all alive and together then, my father and mother and all of us; the old shebeen we lived in looked like the skull of a house, it was so old, and the roof falling in on us, but thank God, we were happy in it—Oh, Ireland's the lovely country, sir."

"No bad people at all there?" asked the captain, looking at her kindly.

"Oh, sir, there are then," said the little maid, regretfully. "I have sins upon my own soul, truth I have, sir. The sin of st'aling was my black shame when I was growing up, then."

"What did you ever steal, child?" asked the captain.

"Mostly eggs, sir," said Nora, humbly.

"I dare say you were hungry," said the old man, taking up his newspaper and pretending to frown at the shipping list.

"Oh, no, captain, 'twas not that always. I used to follow an old spickled hen of my mother's and wait for the egg. I'd track her within the furze, and whin I'd be two days getting two eggs I'd run wid 'em to sell 'em, and 'twas to buy things to sew for me doll I'd spind the money. I'd ought to make confission for it now too. I'm shamed, thinkin' of it, and the spickled hen was one that laid very large white eggs intirely, and whiles my poor mother would be missing them and thinking the old hen was no good and had best be killed, the honest cr'atur', and go to market that way when poulthry was dear. I'd like one of her eggs now to boil it myself for you, sir; 'twould be aisy 'atin' for you coming right in from some place under the green bushes. I think she's long dead, I didn't see her a long while before I was l'avin'. A woman called Johanna Spillane bought her from my aunt when my mother was dead. She was a very honest, good hen; a top-knot hen, sir."

"I dare say," said the captain, looking at his newspaper; he did not know why the simple chatter touched and pleased him so. He shrugged his shoulders and moved about in his easy chair, frowned still more at the shipping list, and so got the better of his emotion.

"I see that the old brig Miranda has gone ashore on the Florida Keys," he said, as if speaking to a large audience of retired shipmasters. "Stove her bows, rigging cut loose and washed overboard; total wreck. I suppose you never saw a wreck?"—he turned and regarded Nora affectionately.

"I did, sir, then," said Nora Connelly, flushing with satisfaction. "We got news of it one morning early, and all trooped to the shore, every grown person and child in the place, l'aving out Mother Dolan, the ould lady that had no use of her two legs, and all the women, me mother and all, took their babies to her and left them, and she entreatin'—you'd hear the bawls of her a mile away—that some of the folks would take her wid 'em on their backs to see what would she get wid the rest; but we left her screeching wid all the poor shilder, and I was there with the first, and the sun coming up and the ship breaking up fine out a little way in the rocks. 'Twas loaded with sweet oranges, she was, and they all comin' ashore like yellow ducklings in the high wather. I got me fill for once, I did, indeed."

"Dear, dear," said the captain. "Did the crew get ashore?"

"Well, I belave not, sir, but I couldn't rightly say. I was small, and I took no notice. I mind there were strangers round that day, but sailors or the nixt parish was one to me then. The tide was going out soon, and then we swarmed aboard, and, wisha, the old ship tipped up wid us in it, and I thought I was killed. 'Twas a foine vessel, all gilded round the cabin walls, and I thought in vain 'twould be one like her comin' to Ameriky. There was wines aboard, too, and all the men got their fill. Mesilf was gatherin' me little petticoat full of oranges that bobbed in the wather in the down-side of the deck. Wisha, sir, the min were pushin' me and the other shilder into the wather; they were very soon tight, sir, and my own father was wid 'em, God rest his soul! and his cheeks as red as two roses. Some busy body caught him ashore and took him to the magistrate—that was the squire of our place, sir, and an illigant gentleman. The bliguards was holdin' my father, and I running along, screeching for fear he'd be going to jail on me. The old squire began to laugh, poor man, when he saw who it was, and says he, 'Is it yoursilf, Davy?' and says my father, 'It's mesilf, God save your honor, very tight intirely, and feelin' as foine as any lord in Ireland. L'ave me go, and I'll soon slape it off under the next furze-bush that'll stop still long enough for me by the roadside,' says he. The squire says, 'L'ave him go, boys, 'twas all from his 'ating the oranges!' says he, and the folks give a great laugh all round. He was doin' no harrum, the poor man! I run away again to the say, then; I forget was there any more happened that day."

"She must have been a fruiter from the Mediterranean. I can't think what she was doing up there on the west coast, out of her bearings," said the captain.

"Faix, sir, I couldn't tell you where she was from, if it's the ship you mane; but she wint no further than our parish and the Black Rocks. I heard tell of plinty other foine wrecks, but I was to that mesilf."

III

The lengthening days of late winter went slowly by, and at last it was spring and the windows were left open all day in the captain's room. The household had accepted the fact that nobody pleased the invalid as Nora did, and there was no feeling of jealousy; it was impossible not to be grateful to anyone who could invariably spread the oil of sympathy and kindness over such troubled waters. James Reilly and Mrs. Nash often agreed upon the fact that the captain kept all the will he ever had, but little of the good judgment. Yet, in spite of this they took it upon them to argue with him upon every mistaken point. Nora alone had the art of giving a wide berth to dangerous subjects of conversation, and she could twist almost every sort of persistence or aggravation into a clever joke. She had grown very fond of the lonely old man; the instinct toward motherliness in her simple heart was always ready to shelter him from his fancied wrongs, and to quiet him in the darkest hours of fretfulness and pain.

Young Nora Connelly's face had grown thin during the long winter, and she lost the pretty color from her cheeks as spring came on. She was used to the mild air of Ireland, and to an out-of-door life. She could not feel like herself in the close rooms of Captain Balfour's house on Barry Street. By the time that the first daffodils were in bloom on the south terrace, she longed inexpressibly for the open air and used to disappear from even the captain's sight into the garden, where at times she took her turn with the gardeners at spading up the rich soil, and working with a zeal which put to shame their languid efforts. Something troubled the girl, however; she looked older and less happy; sometimes it was very plain to see that she had been crying.

One morning, when she had been delayed unusually with her downstairs work, the captain grew so impatient that he sent Reilly away to find her. Nora quickly set down a silver candlestick and wiped her powdery hands upon her apron as she ran upstairs. The captain was standing in the middle of the floor, scowling like a pirate in a picture book, and even when Nora came in, he did not smile. "I'm going out to take a walk," he said, angrily.

"Come on, then, sir," said Nora. "I'll run for your coat and hat if you'll tell me where—"

"Pooh, pooh! child!" the pacified captain was smiling broadly. "I only want to take a couple of turns here in the hall. You forget how long I've been house-bound. I'm a good deal better; I'll have that meddling Reilly know it, too; and I won't be told what I may do and what I may not."

"'Tis thrue for you, sir," said Nora, amiably. "Steady yourself with my arrum, now, and we'll go to the far end of the hall and back again. 'Twas the docther himself said a while ago that ye'd ought to thry walking more, and 'twas your honor was like to have the life of him. You're a very conthrairy gentleman, if I may be so bold!"

The captain laughed, but the business of dragging his poor heavy foot was more serious than he had expected, in spite of all his brave determination. Nora did her best to beguile him from too much consciousness of his feebleness and disappointment.

"Sure if you'd see ould Mother Killahan come hobbling into church, you'd think yourself as good as a greyhound," she said, presently, while the master rested in one of the chairs at the hall's end. "She's very old intirely. I saw her myself asleep at her beads this morning, but she do be very steady on her two knees, and whiles she prays and says a bead or two, and whiles she gets a bit of sleep, the poor cr'ature. She do be staying in the church a dale this cold weather, and Father Dunn is very aisy with her. She makes the stations every morning of the year, so she does, and one day she come t'rough the deep snow in a great storm there was, and she fell down with weakness on the church steps; and they told Father Dunn and said how would they get her home, and he come running himself scolding all the way and took her up in his arrums, and wint back with her to his own house. You'd thought she was his own mother, sir. 'She's one of God's poor,' says he, with the tears in his eyes. Oh, captain, sir! I wish it was Father Dunn was praste to you, I do then! I'm thinking he'd know what prayers would be right for you, and himself was born in the country forninst Glengariff, and would tell you how foine it was for your stringth. If you'd get better, sir, and we'd meet him on the street, we'd be after asking his riverence."

The captain made no answer, he was tired and spent, and sank into his disdained easy-chair, grateful for its comfortable support. The mention of possible help for his feeble frame from any source clung to his erratic memory, and after a few days one of the thoughts that haunted his mind was that Father Dunn, a kind-faced, elderly man, might be of use in this great emergency. To everybody's surprise, his bodily strength seemed to be slowly returning as the spring days went by, but there was oftener and oftener an appealing, childish look in his face, the firm lines of it were blurred, even while there was a steady renewing of his shattered forces. At last he was able to drive down the busy street one day, with Reilly, in his familiar chaise. The captain's old friends gathered to welcome him, and he responded to their salutations with dignity and evident pleasure; but once or twice, when someone congratulated him upon certain successful matters of business which he had planned before his illness, there was only a troubled look of dulness and almost pain for answer.

One day Nora Connelly stole out into the garden in the afternoon, and sat there idly under an old peach-tree. The green fruit showed itself thick all along the slender boughs. Nora had been crying already, and now she looked up through the green leaves at the far blue sky, and then began to cry again. She was sadly homesick, poor child! She longed for her lover, whom she feared now never to see. Like a picture she recalled the familiar little group of thatched houses at home, with their white walls and the narrow green lanes between; she saw the pink daisies under foot and the golden gorse climbing the hill till it stood against the white clouds. She remembered the figures of the blue-cloaked women who went and came, the barefooted merry children and the dabbling ducks; then she fell to thinking lovingly of her last walk with Johnny

Morris, the empty bird's nest, and all their hopes and promises the night before she left home. She had been wilful in yielding to her aunt's plans; she knew that Johnny feared her faithlessness, but it was all for love of him that she had left him. She knew how poor they were at home. She had faithfully sent a pound a month to her aunt, and though she had had angry appeals for more, the other pound that she could spare, leaving but little for herself, had been sent in secret to Johnny's mother. She always dreaded the day when her avaricious aunt should find this out and empty all the vials of her wrath of covetousness. Nora, to use her own expression, was as much in dread of this aunt as if the sea were a dry ditch. Alas! she was still the same poor Nora Connelly, though rich and busy America stretched eastward and westward from where she had made her new home. It was only by keeping her pounds in her pocket that she could gather enough to be of real and permanent use to those she loved; and yet their every day woes, real or fictitious, stole the pounds from her one by one.

So she sat crying under the peach-tree until the pale old captain came by, in the box-bordered walk, with scuffling, unsteady steps. He saw Nora and stopped, leaning on his cane.

"Come, come, Nora!" he said, anxiously. "What's the matter, my girl?"

Nora looked up at him and smiled instantly. It was as if the warm Irish sunshine had broken out in the middle of a May shower. A long spray of purple foxglove grew at her feet and the captain glanced down at it. The sight of it was almost more than she could bear, this flower that grew in the hedgerows at home. She felt as if the flower were exiled like herself and trying to grow in a strange country.

"Don't touch it, sir," she faltered, as the captain moved it with his cane; "'tis very bad luck to meddle with that: they say yourself will be meddled with by the fairies. Fairy Fingers is the name of that flower, we were niver left pick it. Oh, but it minds me of home."

"What's the matter with you to-day?" asked the captain.

"I've been feeling very sad, sir, I can't help it either, thinkin' o' me home I've left and me dear lad that I'll see no more. I was wrong to l'ave him, I was indeed."

"What lad?" asked Captain Balfour, suspiciously, "I'll have no nonsense nor lads about my place. You're too young—"He looked sharply at the tearful young face. "Mrs. Nash can't spare you either," he added, humbly, in a different tone.

"Faix, sir, it's at home he is, in the old country, without me; he'll niver trouble ye, me poor Johnny," Nora explained, sadly enough. She had risen with proper courtesy, and was standing by the old man; now she ventured to take hold of his arm. He looked flushed and eager, and she forgot herself in the instinct to take care of him.

"Where do you be going so fast?" she asked, with a little laugh. "I'm afther believing 'tis running away you are."

The captain regarded her solemnly, then he laughed too. "Come with me," he said. "I'm going to make a call."

"Where would it be?" demanded the girl, with less than her usual deference.

"Come, come! I want to be off," insisted the old gentleman. "We'll go out of this little gate in the fence. I've got to see your Father Dunn on a matter of business," he said, as if he had no idea of accepting any remonstrance.

Nora knew that the doctor and all the elder members of the household approved of her master's amusing himself and taking all the exercise he could. She herself approved his present intentions entirely; it was not for her to battle with the head of the house, at any rate, so she dutifully and with great interest and anxiety set forth beside him down the path, on the alert for any falterings or missteps.

They went out at the gate in the high fence, the master remembered where to find the key, and he seemed in excellent spirits. The side street led them down the hill to Father Dunn's house, but when they reached it the poor captain was tired out. Nora began to be frightened as she stole a look at him. She had forgotten, in the pride of her own youthful strength, that it would be such a long walk for him. She was anxious about the interview with Father Dunn, she had no idea how to account for their presence, but she had small opinion of the merits and ability of the captain's own parish minister, and felt confident of the good result, in some way, of the visit. Presently the priest's quick step was heard in the passage, Nora rose dutifully as he came in, but was only noticed by a kindly glance. The old captain tried to rise too, but could not, and Father Dunn and he greeted each other with evident regard and respect. Father Dunn sat down with a questioning look, he was a busy man with a great parish, and almost everyone of his visitors came to him with an important errand.

The room was stiff-looking and a little bare, everything in it was well worn. There was a fine portrait of Father Dunn's predecessor, or, it should rather be said, a poor portrait of a fine man whose personal goodness and power of doing Christian service shone in his face. Father Miles had been the first priest in that fast-growing inland town, and the captain had known and respected him. He did not say anything now, but sat looking up much pleased at the picture. This parlor of the priest's house had a strangely public and impersonal look, it had been the scene of many parish weddings and christenings, and sober givings of rebuke and kindly counsel. Nora gazed about her with awe, she had been brought up in great reverence of holy things and of her spiritual pastors and masters; but she could not help noticing that the captain was a little astray in these first few moments. There stole in upon his pleased contemplation of the portrait a fretful sense of doing an unaccustomed thing, and he could not regain his familiar dignity and self-possession; that conscious right to authority which through long years had stood him in such good stead. He was only a poor broken-down, sick old man; he had never quite understood the truth about himself before, and the thought choked him, he could not speak.

"The masther was coveting to spake with your riverence about Glengariff," ventured Nora, timidly, feeling at last that the success of the visit depended wholly upon herself.

"Oh, Glengariff, indeed!" exclaimed the good priest, much relieved. He had discovered the pathetic situation at last, and his face grew compassionate.

"This little girl seems to believe that it would set me up to have a change of air. I haven't been very well, Father Dunn." The captain was quite himself again for the moment, as he spoke. "You may not have heard that the doctors have had hold of me lately? Nora, here, has been looking after me very well, and she speaks of some sea-bathing on your Irish coast. I may not be able to leave my business long enough to do any good. It's going to the dogs, at any rate, but I've got enough to carry me through."

Nora was flushing with eagerness, but the priest saw how white the old captain's fingers were, where they clasped his walking-stick, how blurred and feeble his face had grown. The thought of the green hills and hollows along the old familiar shore, the lovely reaches of the bay, the soft air, the flowery hedgerows, came to his mind as if he had been among them but yesterday.

"I wish that you were there, sir, I do indeed," said Father Dunn. "It is nearer like heaven than any spot in the world to me, is old Glengariff. You would be pleased there, I'm certain. But you're not strong enough for the voyage, I fear, Captain Balfour. You'd best wait a bit and regain your strength a little more. A man's home is best, I think, when he's not well."

The captain and Nora both looked defeated. Father Dunn saw their sadness, and was sure that his kindest duty was to interest this poor guest and to make a pleasure for him, if possible.

"I can tell you all about it, sir, and how you might get there," he went on hastily, shaking his head to someone who had come to summon him. "Land at Queenstown, go right up to Cork and pass the night, and then by rail and coach next day—'tis but a brief journey and you're there. 'Tis a grand little hotel you'll find close to the bay—'twas like a palace to me in my boyhood, with the fine tourists coming and going; well, I wish we were there this day and I showing you up and down the length of the green country."

"Just what I want—I've been a busy man, but when I take a holiday give me none of your noisy towns," said the captain, eager and cheerful again.

"You'd be so still there that a bird lighting in the thatch would wake you," said Father Dunn. "Ah, 'tis many a long year since I saw the place. I dream of it by night sometimes, Captain Balfour, God bless it!"

Nora could not keep back the ready tears. The very thought that his reverence had grown to manhood in her own dear country side was too much for her.

"You're not thinking of going over this summer?" asked the captain, wistfully. "I should be gratified if you would bear me company, sir, I'd try to do my part to make it pleasant." But the good father shook his head and rose hastily, to stand by the window that looked out into his little garden.

"We'd make a good company," said he, presently, turning toward them and smiling, "with young Nora here to show us our way. You can't have had time yet, my child, to forget the old roads across country!" and Nora fairly sobbed.

"Pray for the likes of me, sir!" she faltered, and covered her face with her hands. "Oh, pray for the masther too, your riverence Father Dunn, sir; 'tis very wake he is, and 'tis mesilf that's very lonesome in Ameriky an' I'm afther l'aving the one I love!"

"Be quiet, now!" said the priest, gravely, checking her with a kindly touch of his hand, and glancing at Captain Balfour. The poor old man looked in a worried way from one to the other, and Father Dunn went away to fetch him a glass of wine. Then he was ready to go home, and Father Dunn got his hat and big cane, pleading that an errand was taking him in the same direction.

"If I thought it would do me any good, I would start for that place we were speaking of to-morrow," said the captain as they set forth. "You know to what I refer, the sea-bathing and all." The priest walked slowly, the captain's steps grew more and more faltering and unsteady. Nora Connelly followed anxiously. There flitted through Father Dunn's mind phrases out of the old Bible story—"a great man and honorable"—"a valiant man and rich," "but a leper" —the little captive maid that brought him to the man of God. Alas, Father Dunn could tell the captain of no waters of Jordan that would make him a sound man he could only say to him——: Go in peace, like the prophet of old.

When they reached home the household already sought for the captain in despair, but it happened that nobody was in the wide, cool hall as they entered.

"I hope that you will come in and take a glass of wine with me. You have treated me with brotherly kindness, sir," said the master of the house; but Father Dunn shook his head and smiled as he made the old man comfortable in a corner of the broad sofa, taking his hat and stick from him and giving them to Nora. "Not to-day, Captain Balfour, if you will excuse me."

The captain looked disappointed and childish. "I am going to send you a bottle of my father's best old madeira," he said. "Sometimes, when a man is tired out or has a friend come in to dine—"But he was too weary himself to finish the sentence. The old house was very still, there were distant voices in the garden, a door at the end of the hall opened into an arbor where flickers of light were shining through the green vine leaves. Everything was stately and handsome, there was a touch everywhere of that colonial elegance of the captain's grandfather's time which had never been sacrificed to the demon of change, that restless American spirit which has spoiled the beauty of so many fine and simple old houses.

The priest was used to seeing a different sort of household interior, his work was among the poor. Then he looked again at the house's owner, an old man, sick, sorry, and alone. "God bless you, sir," he said. "I must be going now."

"Come and see me again," said the captain, opening his eyes. "You are a good man, I am glad to have your blessing." The words were spoken with a manly simplicity and directness that had always been liked by Captain Balfour's friends. "Nora," he whispered, when Father Dunn had gone, "we'll say nothing to Mrs. Nash. I must rest a little while here before we get up the stairs."

IV

Toward the end of the summer things had grown steadily worse, and Captain Balfour was known to be failing fast. The clerks had ceased to come for his signature long before; he had forgotten all about business and pleasure too, and slept a good deal, and sometimes was glad to see his friends and sometimes indifferent to their presence. But one day, when he felt well enough to sit in his great chair by the window, he told Mr. Barton, his good friend and lawyer, that he wished to attend to a small matter of business. "I've arranged everything long ago as an aging man should," he said. "I don't know that there's any hurry, but I'll mention this item while I think of it. Nora, you may go downstairs," he said sharply to the girl, who had just entered upon an errand of luncheon or medicine, and Nora disappeared; she remembered afterward that it was the only time when, of his own accord and seeming impatience, he had sent her away.

Reilly and Mrs. Nash bore no ill will toward their young housemate, they were reasonable enough to regard Captain Balfour's fondness for her with approval. There was something so devoted and single-hearted about the young Irish girl that they had become fond of her themselves. They had their own plans for the future, and looked forward to being married when the captain should have no more need of them. It really hurt Mrs. Nash's feelings when she often found Nora in tears, for the desperate longing for home and for Johnny Morris grew worse in the child's affectionate heart instead of better.

One day Mr. Reilly had gone down town, leaving the captain asleep. Nora was on guard, Mrs. Nash was at hand in the next room with her sewing, and Nora sat still by the window; the captain was apt to sleep long and heavily at this time of the day. She was busy with some crocheting, it was some edging of a pattern that the sisters of Kenmare had taught Johnny Morris's mother. She gave a little sigh at last and folded her hands in her lap, her gray Irish eyes were blinded with tears.

"What's the matter, child?" asked the captain, unexpectedly; his voice sounded very feeble.

Nora started, she had forgotten him and his house.

"Will you have anything, sir?" she asked, anxiously.

"No, no, what's the matter, child?" asked the old man kindly.

"'Tis me old story; I'm longing for me home and I can't help it if I died too. I'm like a thing torn up by the roots and left in the road. You're very good, sir, and I would never l'ave the house and you in it, but 'tis home I think of by night and by day; however will I get home?"

Captain Balfour looked at her compassionately. "You're a good girl, Nora; perhaps you'll go home before long," he said.

"'Tis sorra a few goes back; Ameriky's the same as heaven for the like o' that," answered Nora, trying to smile and drying her eyes. "There's many'd go back too but for the presents every one looks to have; 'twould take a dale of money to pl'ase the whole road as you pass by. 'Tis a kind of fever the young ones has to be l'aving home. Some l'aves good steady work and home and friends, that might do well. There's getting to be fine chances for smart ones there with so many l'aving."

"Yes, yes," said the captain. "We'll talk that over another time, I want to go to sleep now;" and Nora flushed with shame and took up her crocheting again. "'Twas me hope of growing rich, and me aunt's tongue shaming me that gets the blame," she murmured to herself. The sick man's hands looked very white and thin on the sides of his chair; she looked at them and at his face, and her heart smote her for selfishness. She was glad to be in America, after all.

They never said anything to each other now about going to Glengariff, a good many days slipped by when the captain hardly spoke except to answer questions; but in restless evenings, when he could not sleep, people who passed by in the street could hear Nora singing her old familiar songs of love and war, sometimes in monotonous plaintive cadences that repeated and repeated a refrain, sometimes in livelier measure with strange thrilling catches and prolonged high notes, as a bird might sing to its mate in the early dawn out in the wild green pastures. The lovely weird songs of the ancient Irish folk, how old they are, how sweet they are, who can tell? but now and then a listener of this new world of the western seas hears them with deep delight, hears them with a strange golden sense of dim remembrance, a true far-descended birthright of remembrance that can only come from inheritance of Celtic blood.

When the frost had fallen on the old garden, Captain Balfour died and his year of trouble was ended. Reilly and Mrs. Nash, the cook and Nora, cried bitterly in the kitchen, where the sudden news found them. Nobody could wish him to come back, but they cried the more when they thought of that. There was a great deal said about him in the newspapers; about his usefulness in town and state, his wealth, his character, and his history; but nobody knew so well as this faithful household how comfortable he had made his lonely home for other people; and those who knew him best thought most of his kindness, his simple manliness, and sincerity of word and deed.

The evening after the funeral Nora was all alone in her little room under the high roof. She sat on the broad seat of a dormer window where she could look far out over the city roofs to a glimpse of the country beyond. There was a new moon in the sky, the sunset was clear, the early autumn weather was growing warm again.

The old house was to belong to a nephew of the captain, his only near relative, who had spent a great many years abroad with an invalid wife; it was to be closed for the present, and Mrs. Nash and Mr. Reilly were to be married and live there all winter, and then go up country to live in the spring, where Mrs. Nash owned a little farm. She was of north of Ireland birth, was Mrs. Nash; her first husband had been an American. She told Nora again and again that she might always have a home with her, but the fact remained that Nora must find herself a new place, and she sat in the window wondering with a heavy heart what was going to happen to her. All the way to the burying ground and back again in the carriage, with the rest of the household, she had sobbed and mourned, but she cried for herself as much as for the captain. Poor little Irish Nora, with her warm heart and her quick instincts and sympathies! how sadly she thought now of the old talk about going to Glengariff; she had clung long to her vain hope that the dream would come true, and that the old captain and his household were all going over seas together, and so she should get home. Would anybody in America ever be so kind again and need her so much as the captain?

Someone had come to the foot of the stairs and was calling Nora loudly again and again. It was dark in the upper entryway, however bright the west had looked just now from her window; she left her little room in confusion, she had begun already to look over her bits of things, her few clothes and treasures before she packed them to go away. Mrs. Nash seemed to be in a most important hurry and said that they were both wanted in the dining-room, and it was very pleasant somehow to be wanted and made of consequence again. She had begun to feel like such an unnecessary stray little person in the house.

The lamps were lighted in the handsome old dining-room, it was orderly and sedate; one who knew the room half expected to see Captain Balfour's fine figure appear in the doorway to join the waiting group. There were some dark portraits on the wall, and the old Balfour silver stood on the long sideboard. Mrs. Nash had set out all the best furnishings, for this day when the master of the house left it forever.

There were not many persons present and Nora sat down, as someone bade her, feeling very disrespectful as she did it. Mr. Barton, the lawyer, began to read slowly from a large folded paper; it dawned presently upon Nora that this was the poor captain's will. There was a long bequest to the next of kin, there were public gifts, and gifts to different friends, and handsome legacies to faithful Mrs. Nash and James Reilly, and presently the reading was over. There was something quite grand in listening to this talk of thousands and estates, but little Nora, who had no call, as she told herself, to look for anything, felt the more lonely and friendless as she listened. There was a murmur of respectful comment as the reading ended, but Mr. Barton was opening another paper, a small sheet, and looked about him, expecting further attention.

"I am sure that no one will object to the carrying out of our deceased friend's wishes as affirmed in this more recent memorandum. Captain Balfour was already infirm at the time when he gave me the directions, but, as far as I could judge, entirely clear in his mind. He dictated to me the following bequest and signed it. The signature is, I own, nearly illegible, but I am sure that, under the somewhat affecting circumstances, there will be no opposition.

"I desire," read Mr. Barton slowly, "I desire the executors of my will to pay five hundred dollars within one month after my death to Nora Connelly, also to secure her comfortable second-class passage to the port of Queenstown, in Ireland. I mean that, if she still desires, she may return to her home. I am sensible of her patience and kindness and I attempt in this poor way to express my gratitude to a good child. I wish her a safe return and that every happiness may attend her future life.

"JOHN BALFOUR"

"'Tis a hundred pounds for ye an' yer passage, me darlin'," whispered the cook, excitedly. "'Tis mesilf knew you wouldn't be forgotten an' the rist of us so well remimbered. 'Tis foine luck for ye; Heaven rist his soul, the poor captain!"

Nora was sitting pale and silent. She did not cry now, her heart was deeply touched, her thoughts flew homeward. She seemed to hear the white waves breaking about the ship, and to see the far deep colors of the Irish shore. For Johnny had said again and again that if they had a hundred pounds and their two pairs of hands, he could do as well with his little farm as any man in Ireland.

❧

"Sind for your lad to come over," urged Cousin Donahue, a day later, when the news had been told; but Nora proudly shook her head. She had asked for her passage the very next week. It was a fine country, America, for those with the courage for it, but not for Nora Connelly, that had left her heart behind her. Cousin Donahue laughed and shook his head at such folly, and offered a week's free lodging to herself and Johnny the next spring, when she'd be the second time a greenhorn coming over. But Nora laughed too, and sailed away one Saturday morning in late October, across the windy sea to Ireland.

V

Again it was gray twilight after a short autumn day in the old country, and a tall Irish lad was walking along the highroad that led into Kenmare. He was strong and eager for work, but his young heart was heavy within him. The piece of land which he held needed two men's labor, and work as he might, he must fall behind with his rent. It was three years since that had happened before, and he had tried so hard to do well with his crops, and had even painfully read a book that was wise about crops which the agent had lent him, and talked much besides with all the good farmers. It was no use, he could not hold his own, times were bad and sorrowful, and Nora was away. He had believed that, whatever happened to her fortunes, he should be able in time to send for her himself and be a well-off man. Oh, for a hundred pounds in his pocket to renew his wornout land! to pay a man to help him with the new ditching—oh, for courage to fight his way to independence on Irish ground. "I've only got my heart and my two hands, God forgive me!" said Johnny Morris, aloud. "God be good to me and Norry, and me poor mother! Maybe I'll be after getting a letter from me darling the night, 'tis long since she wrote."

He stepped back among the bushes to let a side-car pass that had come up suddenly behind him. He recognized the step of Dinny Killoren's fast pacer, and looked to see if there were room on the car for another passenger, or if perhaps Dinny might be alone and glad to have company. There was only Dinny himself and a woman who gave a strange cry. The pacer stopped and Johnny's heart beat within him as if it would come out of his breast. "My God, who's this?" he said.

"Lift me down, lift me down!" said the girl. "Oh, God be thanked, I'm here!" and Johnny leaped forward and caught Nora Connelly in his arms.

"Is it yoursilf?" he faltered, and Nora said, "It's mesilf indeed, then." And Dinny Killoren laughed aloud on the side-car, with his pacer backing and jumping and threatening to upset all Nora's goods in the road. There was a house near by, a whiff of turf smoke, drifting low in the damp air, blew into Nora's face; she heard the bells begin to ring in Kenmare. It was the evening of a saint's day and they rang and rang, and Nora had come home.

So she married the lad she loved, and was a kind daughter to his mother. They spent a good bit of the captain's money on their farm, and gave it a fine start, and were able to flaunt their prosperity in the face of that unkind aunt who had wished to make them spend their lives apart. They were seen early on market days in Kenmare, and Nora only laughed when foolish young people said that the only decent country in the world was America. Sometimes she sat in her doorway in the long summer evening and thought affectionately of Captain Balfour, the poor, kind gentleman, and blessed herself devoutly. Often she said a prayer for him on Sunday morning as she knelt in the parish church, with flocks of blackbirds singing outside among the green hedges, under the lovely Irish sky.

Sources

"Spring Sowing" by Liam O'Flaherty. From *The Best British Stories of 1924,* edited by Edward J. O'Brien and John Cournos (Small, Maynard & Company, 1924).

"The Faction Fight" by Frank Mathew. From *At the Rising of the Moon* (McClure & Company, 1893).

"Some Parishioners," by George Moore. From *The Untilled Field* (William Heinemann Publishers: 1914).

"The Gombeen Man," by Bram Stoker. From *The Snake's Pass* (Sampson Low, Marston, Searle & Rivington, Ltd, 1891).

"The Wonderful Tune," by T. Crofton Croker. From *Fairy Legends and Traditions of the South of Ireland* (Lea and Blanchard, 1844).

"The Irishman Abroad," by George A. Birmingham. From *Connaught to Chicago* (Birmingham, 1914).

"James O'Rourke's First Day in New York," by John McElgun. From *Annie Reilly* (J.A. McGee Publishers, 1873).

"Boyne Water and Bad Blood," and "The Freedom Picnic," by Finley Peter Dunne. From *Mr. Dooley In the Hearts of His Countrymen* (Small, Maynard & Company, 1899).

"The Green Flag," by Arthur Conan Doyle. From *The Green Flag and Other Stories of War and Sport.* (McClure, Phillips & Co., 1900).

"O'Reilly's Great Escape," by Alexander Young. From *John Boyle O'Reilly, His Life, Poems and Speeches* (Cassell Publishing, 1891).

"Village Ghosts," by William Butler Yeats. From *Fairy and Folk Tales of the Irish Peasantry* (Walter Scott, 1888).

"Donald and His Neighbors," *Hibernian Tales.* From *The Irish Sketch Book and Critical Review* by William M. Thackeray (Smith, Elder & Co., 1879).

"A Rich Woman" by Katharine Tynan. From *An Isle in the Water* (Adam and Charles Black, 1895).

"Penelope's Irish Experiences," by Kate Douglas Wiggin. From *Penelope's Irish Experiences* (Houghton, Mifflin and Company, 1901).

"Oisin and Patrick," by Lady Gregory. From *Gods and Fighting Men* (John Murray Publisher, 1910).

"The Gaelic Concert," by Ellis N. Myles. From *The Irish World Newspaper,* August 1924.

"The Battle of the Berrins," by Samuel Lover. From *The Novels and Tales of Samuel Lover, Volume IV.* (George Routledge and Sons, 1870).

"The Red Pony," transcribed/translated by William Larminie. From *West Irish Folk-Tales and Romances* (The Camden Library, Elliot Stock, 1893).

"A Little Captive Maid" by Sarah Orne Jewett. From *Scribner's Magazine,* December 1891.